SHAMANIC
MYSTERIES
OF
PERU

D1496494

"Few books on shamanic traditions transmit ancient knowledge the way this one does. It is a sacred artifact with the capacity to unveil hidden wisdom of the Incas. For those who want to unlock such mysteries, for the bold and adventurous reader, and even for the curious bookworm, open your heart and mind and prepare yourself for an intimate spiritual journey."

KRISTIN MARIE HARRIS, PH.D., RESEARCHER OF ESOTERIC
TRADITIONS IN SOUTH AND MESOAMERICA,
AND ALLAN COMBS, PH.D.,
AUTHOR OF *CONSCIOUSNESS EXPLAINED BETTER*

"An extraordinary book that will have every reader feeling deeply connected to and transformed by the spiritual wisdom of the Andean people. With grace and beauty, Lopez and Star Wolf share fascinating teachings garnered through three decades of facilitating magical and mystical journeys to the area. This book will open your heart, expand your consciousness, and light the way to a more peaceful way of *being*."

TAMMY BILLUPS, AUTHOR OF *ANIMAL SOUL CONTRACTS*

"In this beautiful and inspiring work, the authors share a call to remember an important spiritual legacy. Most importantly, this book contains a transmission of the deep feminine wisdom of the Q'eros nation, whose vision and rooted earth connection with the Earth Mother is needed now more than ever. Every page is a pilgrimage, taking you on a mystical and heart-opening journey of remembrance."

SEREN BERTRAND & AZRA BERTAND, M.D., AUTHORS OF
WOMB AWAKENING AND *MAGDALENE MYSTERIES*

"What wonderful gifts *Shamanic Mysteries of Peru* gives us! The authors take the reader on a magical journey to access the wisdom and love of the Q'eros people, who have held on to their 5th dimensional frequency and have so much wisdom to help heal our world. This is a must-read for all spiritual seekers."

JUDITH CORVIN-BLACKBURN, LCSW, DMIN., AUTHOR OF
ACTIVATING YOUR 5D FREQUENCY

"Star Wolf and Vera have adeptly opened the doors to the inner sanctuary of the mysteries of Peru, inviting the reader on a path of transformation, alignment, and coming home. *Shamanic Mysteries of Peru* is a profound opportunity of heart-initiation that will contribute to many during the evolution into higher consciousness."

DANIELLE RAMA HOFFMAN,
AUTHOR OF *THE TABLETS OF LIGHT*

"The combination of Vera Lopez's years of saturation in the magical realm of Peru with Star Wolf's decades-long experience with shamanic practices and principles has produced a deeply moving exploration into the mystical foundation of shamanic Peru. This journey is not to be missed!"

RUBY FALCONER, COAUTHOR OF
SHAMANIC EGYPTIAN ASTROLOGY

"The authors share with us the ancestral wisdom of shamanic Peru to heal our heart-mind disconnect and help us move forward with precision and purpose. If you feel called to make a sacred inner or outer journey to the high Andes, this book is your ticket."

THEA SUMMER DEER,
AUTHOR OF *WISDOM OF THE PLANT DEVAS*

"The sacred land of Peru will hold you in its heart as soaring peak meets sky, clouds dance with forests at 13,000 feet, and Condor and Hummingbird soar. The deep, transformative medicine of the land and the wisdom of its people are what our world needs right now. Lopez and Star Wolf lead us on this journey with compassion and insight, guiding us along the path of initiation so that we too may soar!"

ANNA CARIAD-BARRETT, DMin, M.S., MFT,
COAUTHOR OF *SACRED MEDICINE OF BEE,
BUTTERFLY, EARTHWORM, AND SPIDER*

"Taking you on an intimate journey of discovery, the authors share their personal experiences of one of the world's most enigmatic power centers. From exploring the Serpent of Light and the feminine energy rising from the Andes, you will gain deep knowledge and wisdom with every page that is turned. A new best seller!"

MARIA WHEATLEY, FOUNDER OF ESOTERIC COLLEGE
AND AUTHOR OF *DRUIDIC SOUL STAR ASTROLOGY*

SHAMANIC MYSTERIES OF PERU

THE HEART WISDOM OF THE HIGH ANDES

VERA LOPEZ and
LINDA STAR WOLF, PH.D.

Bear & Company
Rochester, Vermont

Bear & Company
One Park Street
Rochester, Vermont 05767
www.BearandCompanyBooks.com

SUSTAINABLE FORESTRY INITIATIVE   Certified Sourcing
www.sfiprogram.org
SFI-00854

Text stock is SFI certified

Bear & Company is a division of Inner Traditions International

Cataloging-in-Publication Data for this title is available from the Library of Congress

ISBN 978-1-59143-374-3 (print)
ISBN 978-1-59143-375-0 (ebook)

Printed and bound in the United States by Lake Book Manufacturing, Inc.
The text stock is SFI certified. The Sustainable Forestry Initiative® program
promotes sustainable forest management.

10 9 8 7 6 5 4 3 2 1

Text design Virginia Scott Bowman and layout by Priscilla Baker
This book was typeset in Garamond Premier Pro with Transcend and Futura used
as display typefaces

To send correspondence to the author of this book, mail a first-class letter
to the author c/o Inner Traditions • Bear & Company, One Park Street,
Rochester, VT 05767, and we will forward the communication, or contact
Vera Lopez directly at **www.spiritsoftheearth.com**
and Linda Star Wolf at **www.shamanicbreathwork.org**.

This book is dedicated to the Children of the Sun.

PERU

Lima

Aguas Calientes
Machu Picchu ● ● Ollantaytambo
                ● Moray
Cuzco ● ● Pisac

Paracas Peninsula

ICA
REGION

BOLIVIA

Lake Titicaca

La Paz

Tiwanaku

CONTENTS

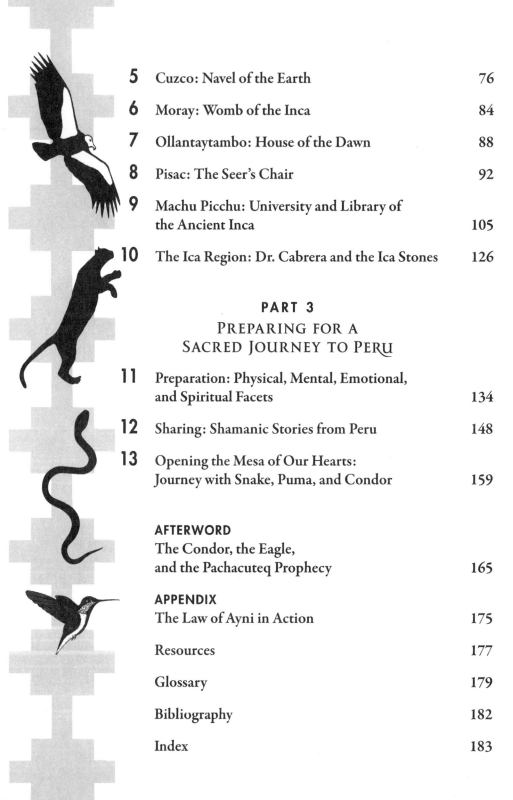

FOREWORD

OUR EARTH IS CURRENTLY in a major evolutionary shift, which is causing an increase in the frequency of its vibrational field. The ancient prophecy of the Americas speaks of this age as one when two great totems of its culture, Eagle and Condor, will come together to birth a reunion of the entire human race in what is predicted to be a great spiritual awakening, and a rapid, exponential paradigm shift of our consciousness.

With this comes resistance, as these changes—which are akin to the quickening that happens when a new birth is imminent—can feel quite chaotic. A realignment takes place as our assemblage point reconfigures. This is supported by our return to the sacred and a remembering of our connection to our mystical shamanic wisdom.

Peru is a country steeped in esoteric wisdom of the heart as maintained by the shamanic traditions of the Q'eros nation that resides in the upper reaches of the Andes Mountains. These traditions and their associated mysteries have existed from time immemorial and today are awakening in the collective consciousness of the world. As such, we are all being called to remember our sacred contract and support the Earth through this shift of the ages. *Shamanic Mysteries of Peru* is a gift for humanity, given that it provides us with a road map to help us navigate the new terrain in which we unexpectedly find ourselves at this time.

With this book, Vera Lopez and Star Wolf connect us to the sacred land of Peru, where the Serpent of Light has awakened the kundalini energy of the feminine life force lying inside our Earth Mother's body.

This life-force energy is calling for a return of the feminine to its rightful place—the heart. This will lead us into a new age of consciousness during which we will be tasked with integrating the healthy masculine and feminine in order to bring forth the golden age.

In this book you will learn many things, including the power of the archetypal animals of the ancient Peruvian culture; these archetypal animals include the condor, the serpent, the hummingbird, and the puma. You will also learn the shamanic axioms and spiritual components that undergird and permeate this unique culture today. They include *karpay* (shamanic initiation), Pachamama (Earth Mother), *ayni* (sacred law of reciprocity), the Chakana (symbol of Andean cosmology), and more.

Peru called to me long ago but it took a channeler to make me aware of this. In 2011 I had a soul reading done by an intuitive, hoping for confirmation about a trip I was intending to take to South Africa. I had never had such a reading before and was not sure what to expect. I was curious what would be revealed about my soul's path.

The backstory is as follows. In 2011, I had done some Shamanic Breathwork. For those of you who don't know, Shamanic Breathwork is a tool developed by Linda Star Wolf wherein one uses the breath, drumming, and chakra-attuned music for healing and transformation. One can enter into altered states of consciousness to receive messages, inspiration, and directives. In the process of engaging in this breathwork, I encountered the vision of a white lion named Marah, who is, in fact, a real lion. Marah was born on December 25, 2000, in the town of Bethlehem, South Africa. Her birth had been prophesied by indigenous elders to usher in the new age. In my breathwork session, Marah appeared and told me that I needed to go to South Africa, which was a bit daunting to hear.

Thus I sought the services of the channeler. "You are traveling over the waters," she said when I asked her about the trip to South Africa. I was in awe that she knew this.

Then she added, "You are going to Peru."

I was stunned and thought, *What? No, I'm going to Africa!* She looked more deeply into my soul and found confirmation for my

African journey but ended our session with the words, "Your soul is strongly calling you to Peru."

I heard her.

I doubted.

And then I trusted.

Soon thereafter I signed up for a shamanic journey to Peru, and following this another Shamanic Breathwork journey confirmed for me the connection between Peru and Africa. I was also informed in the breathwork that my personal and collective work for humanity included my traveling to both of these places.

In March 2012, I traveled to Timbavati, South Africa, to the White Lion Global Protection Trust. Then in December I made the journey to the Sacred Valley of Peru as well as Machu Picchu, a spiritual sanctuary in Peru's Andean Mountains. The trip was led by three incredible shamanic guides: Vera Lopez, Linda Star Wolf, and the late Brad Collins. In Peru, the people of ancient Inca are connected to Pachamama, our Earth Mother. Here our ancestors are in close relationship with the cycles of nature, living in tune with the sun, moon, stars, and earth beings.

In the sacred land of Peru we remembered our connection to the Milky Way and to our star brothers and sisters. We also remembered our connection to Serpent, Puma, and Condor, and to the lower, middle, and upper worlds that are our brothers and sisters as well.

We remembered that natural sites like mountains, rivers, and valleys were where temples had been built to hold the energy of the place, for they connect with the vibrational current of Earth's energetic body. Over time they take on the intentions, prayers, and holiness that have been observed there throughout Earth's history. They become important Earth altars—energy vortexes—carrying highly charged energies of healing and transformation.

Being in the energies of these holy sites in the Sacred Valley was profound. As you will read in chapters 6, 7, and 8, we traveled to the Temples of Moray, Ollantaytambo, and Pisac. And of course we visited Machu Picchu (as discussed in chapter 9).

Each of these experiences helped me to reclaim a part of my soul that had been lost through lineages and lifetimes of trauma. At each site I collected another piece of my own DNA remembrance and true birthright as a divine human.

The Temple of Moray is a sacred site built by the Inca and carved into our Earth like a womb, with concentric circles that descend into a vortex of Pachamama energy. Initially thought to be solely a place of agriculture experimentation, it is now believed that these ruins were also associated with water ceremonies to the gods.

As I walked down the steps of the deepest depression into the largest of these sacred ruins, I felt compelled to take a detour to the left. About halfway down I found myself in the heart of the ruins, the original structure of which had celebrated the Divine Feminine. It too had been built in concentric circles, but it was not as deep as the remainder of the ruins.

I was overcome with waves of emotion that flowed through me as I stepped into its field of energy, for I was feeling an incredibly deep connection with the place and an awakening of the Sacred Feminine at the same time. Tears filled my eyes and my heart swelled with joy as I welcomed her back from what has been her very long absence from this planet.

When I made my way to the ruins dedicated to the masculine energies of our Earth, I joined Star Wolf and Brad in a circle in order to observe a moment of celebration. We had joyous smiles on our faces as we honored what felt to us like a healing of the masculine and feminine energies at the Temple of Moray and throughout the world. And finally there was Machu Picchu, where, on 12-12-12, Vera Lopez, Star Wolf, and Brad Collins, along with Q'eros shamans, conducted a ceremony at sunrise with the energies of this sacred time washing over and around us.

Each site visitation created a cascade of primordial remembering and reclamation for me and no doubt for everyone who was on that journey to Peru in 2012. You too may feel called to undertake a holy pilgrimage to the Sacred Valley and some of the different spiritual sites of Peru. I hope you do, for it will bring about a higher voltage of energy to support humanity as it shifts upward to the next octave of consciousness.

With deep gratitude, I invite you to explore these teachings that furthered my personal journey as spiritual midwife for the Earth and all of her inhabitants.

CARLEY MATTIMORE

CARLEY MATTIMORE is coauthor, with Linda Star Wolf, of *Sacred Messengers of Shamanic Africa*. She is also the cofounder of the Aahara Spiritual Community of Venus Rising in Springfield, Illinois, as well as being a shamanic minister; master Shamanic Breathwork facilitator; Lionhearted Leadership practitioner; and graduate of the White Lion Leadership Academy in South Africa.

THE CALLING OF CHUMA

High Priestess of Machu Picchu

PERU HOLDS A MYSTERY. It holds medicine, and it holds magic.

For several decades, thousands and thousands of people from all over the world have journeyed to the sacred sites and temples of Peru. Each day, over four thousand people walk through the ruins of Machu Picchu. Cuzco, the capital of the Incan Empire, receives just as many visitors, if not more. These tourists take pictures, shop in the local markets, and experience the Peruvian cuisine. For many of them, at the end of the day their journey to Peru is simply a check mark on their world travel list.

Others journey to Peru because they are called. There is a sense, a knowing, a remembrance of a time that has long since passed. These journeyers remember a time when heaven and earth were one. They remember when the land was their teacher and their lover; the animals were their guides and allies. At some deep level, these journeyers—those who are called—remember the shamanic mysteries of Peru, and when they return to this ancient place of power it is not by chance or by accident. It is because they have a date with this land—a date that has been destined by the stars . . .

I have been facilitating shamanic journeys to Peru for over thirty years. With each group and journey, I hear stories from my participants that speak of the magic, the mysteries, and the miracles that transpired and supported them in journeying to Peru. I hear (and tell!) stories of mysterious money manifesting out of thin air, "impossible" vacation time being approved amid a busy production season, logistics of travel and transportation falling effortlessly into place—the list goes on and on. With each story, I smile and know that Peru has called this person to come, and they have listened. With each story I know that another Child of the Sun has returned home once again, and with each story, my heart remembers my own initial journey to Peru . . .

In the late 1980s, I was living in Brazil. I was a banker by trade, and I had lived in Brazil all of my life. I grew up in Brazil, graduated from school in Brazil, and had an established network of family and friends there. Outside of work, I was an active student in an organization called Life and Consciousness. This organization was founded by the world-famous Brazilian medium Luiz Gasparetto, and it was dedicated to studying spirituality and psychology. As a group of about fifty people, we would come together and discover how we could merge both of these fields (spirituality and psychology) together.

In one of our sessions, somebody suggested to our group that we all journey to Machu Picchu. Immediately, all of us said "yes!" to the journey, and we began to plan it. We decided when we would leave, how long we would stay, and what places we would journey to while we were there.

As I left our session, I was overwhelmed with energy and an array of thoughts. I was excited to go to Peru, and at the same time, I had no idea how I was going to realistically make this journey—let alone afford it. All I knew was that some deep part of me had committed to going on the trip; I had definitely heard the call.

When I arrived at work the following Monday, my mind was still racing—trying to figure out how I was going to truly afford this journey to Peru I had committed to over the weekend. I sat at my desk, unlocked my drawer, and pulled out my daily paperwork when I discovered an envelope tucked within the contents of my drawer. The envelope was addressed to me, and underneath my name were the words *A Gift*.

Puzzled at how this envelope managed to get inside my locked drawer, I opened it and found twelve brand-new one-hundred-dollar bills tucked neatly inside. I counted and examined each bill. All of them were crisp—brand-new—as if they had just come out of the machine.

At this point, I believed myself to be the target of a joke. I stuffed the bills back inside the drawer and approached my supervisor.

"What the hell is this?" I asked my supervisor. "Did you put this envelope in my drawer? Is this some kind of joke?"

"No," said my supervisor, looking as confused as I was.

When it was apparent that my supervisor had no idea where this money had come from, nor how it had found its way into my desk, I immediately went to the central bank.

As a backdrop to my story, it is important to note that at the time American dollars were not easy to come by if you were living in Brazil. There was a whole process that Brazilians had to go through to request American currency. We had to schedule an appointment at the central bank, supply a series of documents such as our passports and other documents that stated we were traveling to the United States, and then request the amount of funds we required. Acquiring American dollars was by no means an easy feat.

At the central bank I stood in line, waiting for the next available teller, and all the while thinking to myself that the bills must be fake. When my turn arrived, I took one of the hundred-dollar bills from the envelope and approached the bank counter.

"Hello, can you tell me if this bill is fraudulent?" I asked the teller, handing her the bill.

"How did you receive this?" she asked as she took the bill from my hand.

"It was a gift from a friend who recently returned from America," I quickly lied.

The teller marked the bill with her pen, examined it under the light carefully, and declared that it was indeed an authentic one-hundred-dollar bill.

"Thank you," I said, not bothering to hide the tone of shock in my voice. I collected my money, notified my supervisor that I would not be able to return to work, and rushed home to my apartment.

When I got there I immediately purchased my plane tickets and submitted my payment to the group.

What had seemed daunting and impossible only forty-eight hours prior was now my reality. I was going to Peru.

Looking back, I smile at this memory because now I know that when we say yes to something, and we commit fully from our hearts, we can make magic. To this day, I still do not know where this money came from. I have thanked the mysterious source over a thousand times, and over the past thirty-one years I have seen similar magic happen to others when they say "yes!" to Peru's sacred calling.

A few days before I left for Peru, I was visited by my dear friend Dulce. Dulce and I had a deep and powerful connection. As we connected and as I told her about my upcoming journey and the money having appeared in my desk drawer, she pulled out a bag of runes and told me that she felt called to share them with me.

She encouraged me to think of a question and then pull a rune out of the bag.

I closed my eyes, breathed deeply, and found my question, "What is my purpose in going to Peru?"

I reached inside the velvet bag and moved my fingers around the cold stones until I felt one pull me. I grasped it with my fingers and examined its strange markings in the light.

As I did so, my friend announced to me that I had pulled the cleansing rune.

"I'm going to Peru to cleanse my karma?" I scoffed to myself. "How the hell am I going to do that?"

The night before my flight to Peru was scheduled, I dreamed.

In my dream I found myself on top of a mountain that overlooked an ocean of other mountaintops and peaks. As I looked around, I discovered an elegant, marble-top table situated in the center of the mountaintop. I walked over to the table and ran my fingers over its cold surface.

"What are you doing here on top of the mountain?" a voice demanded. I looked around but found no one else around me.

"I am waiting for God," I responded. "He invited me for supper."

After I had announced my purpose, I woke up.

Coming from a Brazilian and Catholic background, it is important for me to distinguish the importance of supper. For Brazilians and Catholics alike, supper is a special meal. It's different from other meals such as lunch and dinner. Supper is a holy meal; it's a sacred act that you share with the Divine. For example, it's traditional to share Christmas Eve supper with your family to honor and recognize the sacredness of the evening.

So in my dream, I found my specific mention of supper to be an important symbol for me to hold and remember.

I lay in bed the rest of the night contemplating its meaning.

The morning quickly came. I loaded my luggage into the taxi-cab, and the driver drove me to the airport. Once I arrived at the airport, I found my way to the specific gate where I connected with the other members of our travel group. Our group consisted of about fifty Brazilian natives, and we were all eager and anxious for our adventure to Peru. None of us could hold or hide our excitement. Our group leader helped us check our luggage and then we were allowed to board the plane. As our flight flew into the air, each of our faces showed signs of anxious uncertainty as we flew off to Peru—unaware of how our lives would be changed forever.

Our group arrived in Lima, the capital of Peru, and we stayed there for a night; the following day we would travel together to Cuzco. In 1989 Lima was home to a large amount of internal political tension as the communist party of Peru, also known as the "Shining Path," grew in force and power. The Túpac Amaru Revolutionary Movement, which began in the early 1980s, was still active—and due to these internal political shifts and upheavals, my first experience of Lima was dark and militant. The streets were filled with police, and an intensity that mirrored the political dynamics filled the air. Due to these dynamics, Lima was not a stopping point for our journey. We awoke the next morning and boarded a flight to Cuzco.

We were all eager to arrive in Cuzco, the capital of the Incan Empire. When we landed at the Cuzco airport, we could tell that our experience from this point onward was going to be interesting and perhaps otherworldly. The airport was small and was reminiscent of the airports depicted in old movies. The bus that came to pick us up was also worn and beaten up, and as we entered Cuzco the locals flocked to our group asking for bread. As we drove throughout the city, it was eerie to see the streets empty; a silence also filled the air. It was clear to us that the ongoing political dynamics had an influence over this city and its people as well.

When the bus arrived at our lodge we were greeted with a warm welcome that dissipated the tension. Shortly after our arrival our tour guides connected with our group and we left for our tour of Cuzco. Due to the size of our group we were divided into two tour buses, and as we reentered Cuzco it felt as if we had entered another world and another dimension. We were able to walk throughout the ancient temple without the distraction of other groups or visitors; it was just our tour guides and our group of fifty wild Brazilians eager to explore and experience the mysteries of this ancient world. Our tour guides knew that our group was comprised of spiritual seekers and they spoke openly about the mystical history of Cuzco's ancient temples. They introduced us to the Incan cosmology, and spoke about Pachamama and the Apus spirits.

By the end of our day we were all experiencing the worst headaches, due to the altitude adjustments, but we were so connected to the ancient magic of the land that we didn't mind. We returned to our lodge and allowed our bodies to acclimate to the altitude shift. After two days of rest and exploration within Cuzco, our group was ready to travel to Aguas Calientes, the town just below the ruins of Machu Picchu.

At the time, Aguas Calientes was little more than a desolate train station inhabited by a handful of local civilians. Our group reserved the only lodge in town that was available. The facility's accommodations were basic and minimal—private quarters replete with cold showers and beds with clean sheets.

Once our group was settled, we made our way to Machu Picchu.

From our lodge, we walked for about thirty minutes on a set of train tracks that took us to the one bus that transported visitors up to Machu Picchu. In the bus we snaked our way along the one-way road leading up to the site of the ruins; it would soon become one of the Seven Wonders of the World.

Once we arrived, we filed out of the bus and walked up the pathway to the entrance. When we made it to the iconic overlook that allows one to take in the ancient site of Machu Picchu, I couldn't help but feel a sense of deep disappointment and dissatisfaction at the site before me.

This is what I paid twelve hundred dollars to come and see? It's nothing but a bunch of old rocks, I thought to myself as my heart dropped. *This is the place where I am supposed to cleanse my karma?*

I was standing on the platform overlooking Machu Picchu and I was disappointed. I couldn't believe I'd spent my magical money just to see a bunch of dirty rocks.

Our group finished for the day and we returned to our lodge. On the bus ride back down to the village, the group decided to return to Machu Picchu early the next morning to witness the sunrise. I sulked back to my room, crawled into bed, and was swallowed to sleep by my disenchantment.

When the following morning arrived, I found myself with a severe case of altitude sickness. While the rest of the group geared up to witness the sunrise on top of Machu Picchu, I was incredibly sick and throwing up.

My disappointment and disillusionment morphed into downright anger directed at God.

"Oh really, God?" I weakly mumbled. "You had me journey all this way just so I could get sick? This is why you brought me here?"

I was so weak from throwing up that I had no choice but to surrender and accept my condition. I lay in bed, sick and disappointed, and feeling as if I had been betrayed by God. Too weak to stay awake, I passed out from physical exhaustion.

Some time had passed before the urge to get sick yet again woke me up. I looked around the room and was shocked to discover a spirit present.

"Get up and go!" the spirit declared.

"Get up and go where?" I asked, then retorted, "To the bathroom?"

The spirit had no sense of humor. She sternly looked at me, pointed to the door, and once again declared, "Get up and go!"

With her second declaration, she placed a visual of Machu

Picchu in my mind's eye, but it looked different from the site I had witnessed the day before. Through her vision, I began to see Machu Picchu surrounded by orbs of flashing light and energy. The sight of this vision was stunning, and I was moved by the beauty I was witnessing. This spirit was showing me the *energy* of Machu Picchu. She was showing me what Machu Picchu had been back in the time of the Inca.

I knew I could no longer argue with this spirit—whoever she was—so I put together the little energy I had, got dressed, and dragged my body to the old train tracks. I had to walk along the tracks for about thirty minutes before I found myself at the old bus station. For me, boarding the bus to Machu Picchu was a miracle; it was a relief to sit down and know that I was on my way to the ancient ruins.

As the bus climbed its way there, I felt a sense of vitality return to my body. I was restored to strength, with a life-giving energy.

When I arrived at the top of Machu Picchu, I found my way into the ruins of the city where I discovered the members of my group standing in tears around our guide and teacher, Luiz Gasparetto. I walked up to them and inquired why everyone was crying.

"Luiz is channeling an entity named Chuma," a younger woman informed me. "She was the high priestess of Machu Picchu."

As I listened to Luiz and his channeling, I was shocked to discover that he was speaking Quechua—the language native to the indigenous people of Peru. As I continued to listen to Chuma, this entity speaking through Luiz, it dawned on me that this entity was the same spirit that had entered my room and demanded that I get up and go to Machu Picchu!

Chuma announced that she would be at the Mother Earth Temple in Machu Picchu at 12:00 p.m. the next day, and there she would facilitate the cleansing ritual.

When Chuma spoke these words through Luiz, a chill ran down my spine and my body was covered with goose bumps. This was why I had come to Peru—I had come to cleanse my karma.

At this point my vitality and strength were heightened, and I felt a connection to a source of energy that was much larger than I was. I was in the middle of a bigger story, and it was unfolding with clarity all around me.

Ignited with passion and fueled by my spiritual connection to Machu Picchu, I found my way to Luiz, who had just completed channeling. "Luiz," I said excitedly, "Let's spend the night at Machu Picchu!"

With a twinkle in his eye he obliged and directed our group to quickly begin our descent down back to our lodge so that we could collect the necessary belongings for our overnight in the heart of Machu Picchu.

Our group gathered clothes, pillows, and blankets. We packed snacks, and together we caught the last bus of the day to Machu Picchu, making it to the ancient ruins just before nightfall. With the dimming light, we found our way to one of the many ancient temples in the city, and we decided to settle there for the night.

Machu Picchu is different at night. In the daytime your senses are stimulated by the sights and sounds that surround you. At night, the spirits of Machu Picchu come alive and they wander throughout their ancient ruins.

As our group settled and established itself within the confines of this temple, Luiz once again began to channel Chuma.

Through Luiz, Chuma downloaded and revealed to us the history of Machu Picchu. She shared with us that Machu Picchu had not been just a city—it was a university where select women came to study the ancient arts of spirituality and to receive initiation into the priesthood. She shared with us that deep below the ancient ruins is an ancient library, and when humanity is ready, this library and its light will be uncovered and revealed—sharing the sciences of the past, the present, and the future with the world.

There came a point in Chuma's channeling where she announced that she wanted to validate her presence and share the gifts of Machu Picchu with our group. "I want you to have the physical experience of Machu Picchu and witness its spirits, so I will give you three signs to validate our presence with you," Chuma spoke through Luiz. "Behold, I give you the music and song of the night."

As soon as she spoke these words, the hoots of owls began to surround us. It was as if thousands of owls had filled the ruins of Machu Picchu. Their sounds and nighttime calls echoed through the ancient stones, piercing our hearts with their music.

After a couple of minutes the owls' hoots subsided and Chuma spoke again through Luiz. "Now I will give you the blessings of the stars. Look up and receive your blessings," Chuma directed us.

Once again, magic happened. The clouds that hovered above and around us began to drift away and our group was immediately in the presence of the thousands of stars that illuminate South America.

We received these celestial transmissions, and then Chuma presented the third blessing to our group. She proclaimed, "Behold the spirits of Machu Picchu and embrace the gifts of the mystical mists," and out of nowhere, from under the ground below and out of the air around us, mist began to surround our group. The mist crept its way around us, seeping up through the cracks in the stones and descending from the skies above. Within minutes we were encased in the thick mists of Machu Picchu. It was magical and scary at the same time; it felt as if we were inside the most enchanted cauldron.

Chuma imparted our group with this final blessing, and reminded us that we would gather again the next day at Pachamama's temple for the karma cleansing ritual. Chuma's spirit left Luiz's body and we remained in the dark night and the deep silence of Machu Picchu—the Avalon of the Inca.

This experience—spending the night within Machu Picchu—was one of the most powerful of my life. Luiz and I curled together in a blanket and allowed our astral bodies to travel to the etheric realms of Machu Picchu. Our spirits were greeted by the spirits of the ancient priests and priestesses of Machu Picchu who had formed a ritual circle in the central plaza. They wore long white robes and danced within the mists while chanting Quechua prayers, evoking the timeless magic of the land. While Luiz and I could not understand the Quechua prayers, they felt familiar to us. Our spirits remained with these beings for the remainder of the evening.

Luiz and I awoke the next morning just before sunrise, and we witnessed the sun emerge through the Gate of the Sun—a temple within the mountaintops of Machu Picchu. The sun's rays illuminated the stones around us, turning them from silver to gold. Luiz and I did not need to say much about our astral experience. We looked at one another and I just asked, "Do you remember?" and he replied, "Yes!" Luiz then added, "We did not go far but the dance was right here in the plaza." I said, "Yes! It was." We both knew we were the only two members from our group of fifty that were able to leave our bodies and join the priestesses and priests. The rest of the group was afraid to sleep so they talked and shared stories throughout the night.

After getting out of the city to refresh ourselves and eat something, we gathered again and made our way through the city to the Mother Earth Temple.

Once we arrived, Luiz began to channel Chuma and we began our karma-cleansing ceremony.

Chuma shared with us that this ceremony had two pathways for us to choose from. She said that some of us could experience this ceremony by staying in Machu Picchu, and others could receive our karmic cleansing by climbing Huayna Picchu—the mountain behind Machu Picchu. Chuma affirmed that, regardless of our decision, the spirits of Machu Picchu would be with us throughout our journey.

Our group began to choose—some stayed within the city ruins and began their ceremony; others made their way to the base of Huayna Picchu.

In my mind, I knew I wanted to stay within the safety of the city. I wanted to explore and experience this ritual here within the ruins. But my heart guided me otherwise. Despite my fear of heights, I found myself at the base of Huayna Picchu—once again, I was the initiate and climbing this mountain was my initiation.

I stared at the path before me and began to wonder how I would ever make it to the top of this mountain. The pathway was narrow and the climb was steep.

Chuma's voice broke through the doubts in my head, and she revealed to me the secrets of this mountain and its journey.

"This mountain holds the test of presence," Chuma guided me. "As in life, if you look behind you, you look into the past, you will lose your balance, and you will fall. If you look too far ahead into the future, you will distract yourself from your next step and you will fall. The key to this mountain, and the key to this earthly realm, is to remain fully within the present moment. Take each step as it comes—don't look back and don't look ahead of you. Remain fully present in your journey and you will make it to the top."

I digested Chuma's words and began my journey.

I climbed Huayna Picchu like a cat. I used my arms and legs to support me. Chuma's guiding words became my mantra as I climbed. Step by step, I made my way up the mountain. Only focusing on the path before me, I began to feel the mountain itself pulling at my energetic field—removing heavy pieces of my past from this lifetime and others.

My karmic cleansing had begun, and I was releasing lifetimes of pain and suffering. My heart was opening, and my soul was becoming lighter. As I climbed I felt as if I were becoming one with the mountain. I was climbing on my hands and knees. Heeding Chuma's direction, I did not dare take my eyes and focus off the earth in front of me. I felt as though I were staring directly into the Earth herself. Doing so filled my awareness with the presence of the present moment. Climbing further, I began to enter an altered state of consciousness. The stone and mountainside before me began to transform into different images and visuals. These visuals reflected experiences from my childhood, specifically painful moments and memories of my mother. Today I know and understand that my mother loved and cared for me to the best of her ability; at the time of this experience, I had not yet reached this greater understanding. I was still living with the feeling that I was not welcomed within my mother's life. Our relationship was challenging and karmic. Deep within my soul I knew that we had shared multiple lifetimes together where we continued to carry and play out this painful narrative and soul contract.

As I climbed, childhood memories flooded my heart and mind. I cried deep tears of pain—pain of rejection, pain of not being wanted, pain from not being kissed, hugged, and loved. As these tears ran down my face, I could feel Mother Earth healing me. I was still holding these resentments against my mother, and as I climbed, Mother Earth was removing them from my heart. With each image and each memory that was released, I felt lighter—and a sense of motherly belonging began to grow within me. To this day I understand that it was Pachamama who was healing my heart and filling me with the motherly energy that I needed. As this nurturing energy filled my heart, I began to feel loved and cared for, and my connection to Mother Earth grew with each movement forward.

I continued to climb and I continued to release. With each focused movement and step I felt freer, and eventually I found myself at the top of the mountain.

There I took in the sight before me and I fell to my knees and began to sob. Extended out before me was the sea of mountaintops—the same image I'd seen in the powerful dream before coming to Peru. I had made it to the mountaintop where God was waiting to serve me supper, and in this moment, I knew my entire life was about to change . . .

When you journey to Peru, and you walk through the temples and their portals, your life changes. You do not go home the same person. In the past thirty-one years, I have facilitated thousands of spiritual seekers through Peru's initiatory doorways. I have supported these seekers in entering into the mysteries—and upon completion, I have witnessed each person radically transform their life.

After my first journey to Peru, I was guided to end my career and dedicate my life to bringing people to Peru. Since then I have been immersed in the shamanic mysteries of Peru. I have shared this journey with thousands of world travelers, and through these years I have had the privilege and honor to study under and work directly with several indigenous shamans and Peruvian wisdom keepers. These teachers and guides have adopted me into their lineage, welcomed me into their families, and imparted generations of Andean tradition to me.

Through this book and its pages, I pass this same wisdom on to you.

The shamanic mysteries of Peru are still alive. They still carry the magic of the Inca, and they hold timely medicine for our modern-day world. As you read this book and take your own journey through Peru throughout these pages, I invite you to open your heart to these mysteries. I invite you to allow them to permeate your heart, your mind, and your soul, and see how your life begins to change when you integrate these traditions into your everyday life.

As you become the initiate and enter into these mysteries, I call upon the Hanan Pacha—the world of the Great Above. I invite Condor to carry you upon its wings, to guide you and share its ancient knowledge and wisdom with you.

I call upon the Ukhu Pacha—the world of the Great Below. I invite Serpent to journey with you and support you as you shed your skins and transform your life.

And I call for the Kay Pacha—the energies of this world and this dimension. I invite Puma to whisper and remind your heart of Peru's ancient magic. May the Great Puma walk with you as a protector and guide, and may your heart be filled with the blessings of this ancient land.

SHAMANIC BLESSINGS,
VERA LOPEZ

ACKNOWLEDGMENTS

THERE ARE TRULY NO WORDS that can express my gratitude to all the people who have journeyed with me to Peru during the past thirty-one years. Each of you has supported my life's purpose and made this book possible. All my *munay* to you.

I have profound love and gratitude for my spiritual mentor, the highest priestess of Machu Picchu—Chuma. Thank you for entering my life, for showing me the way, and for protecting all my groups with your light and love.

To my late spiritual teacher, my first spiritual guide to Peru, and Chuma's channel: Luiz Gasparetto. Your life's work has been the pillar of my life's journey, and your light is a mirror I am forever honored to reflect.

To my Peruvian guides: Pepe Villena, thank you for helping me fall in love with Peru. Boris Cardenas, much appreciation to you for your wisdom and your heart. Kucho, thank you for showing me the hidden treasures of Machu Picchu, introducing me to the beloved spirit of San Pedro, and seeing the Coyarimac within my soul. And Guido Bernal, my soul brother, thank you for your patience and great munay for your people, Pachamama, myself, and our groups. I love you all!

Profound gratitude to all the Q'eros nation for adopting me and trusting me with your medicine and ancient ways.

Muchas gracias to all my beloved teachers: Don Pedrito, Don Pascual, Don Francisco, Dona Juana, and my sweet Sister Bernadina. Each of your devotions to the ancient wisdom, oral traditions, and Pachamama have blessed my life for eternity.

To the natives of Peru who have adopted me as family: Edith Miguel and Erik Mendoza, you both will always hold a special place within my heart; Margpht Carrasco, my *comadre*; Imasumac, my beloved spiritual daughter; Hampi, my goddaughter; Wilber Salas, my compadre; Vilma Castro, my comadre; John Salas, my godson; Miguel Angel, my spiritual son; Lisbeth Castrillom, my prima; Connie Pacheco, my sister; Pablo Seminario, my favorite artist; and Marilu Behar, my sister—thank you all so much for making me feel I belong.

My deep gratitude to Star Wolf, my shamanic Soul Sis Star. Thank you for seeing the value within these ancient mysteries and thank you for your contributions within this book. Thank you for inspiring me to write it, for bringing your own wisdom to its pages by coauthoring with me, and much gratitude for your trust and for introducing me to this publisher. Your generosity touched my heart and blessed my life; thank you!

Big munay and gratitude to everyone at Inner Traditions International for welcoming me into your family and treating this new author with respect and kindness. I so appreciate each and every one of you, and your participation in the creation of this book. Thank you for making it so special. This book is a treasure box that holds thirty-one years of my life's work. Your support has inspired me to give it my extra best.

I am forever grateful for the trust of Carmen Ballestero and the Pax Universalis family of Brazil as well as Rev. Ed Townley and Unity Church of Chicago members. Also, Esateys Stuchiner, Michael Mammina, Madeleine Merentette, Doug and Victoria Allen, Brad Collins, Star Wolf, and Nikólaus Wolf—thank you for your contributions to humankind and for the honor of co-leading journeys to Peru with me.

Munay and gratitude to Norman Hacker, a star-brother, for his blessings as a friend and for godfathering Spirits of the Earth.

My heartfelt and deep gratitude to Jasin Deegan, an angel that connected to the mysteries alongside me. Jasin, your heart and magic made this book real. Only you know the number of hours that it took for me to channel this work onto paper. Without you this book would not be possible. I am forever grateful!

My profound gratitude to my beloved husband, Jim Hostler. Thank you for your unconditional love and amazing support throughout all these years; your love and support has nurtured my work and ministry.

To Pachamama, Taita Inti, Mama Killa, Ch'aska Urqu, Apus, and Apurunas—thank you for reminding me who am I, and that I am always one with you.

VERA LOPEZ
FOUNDER OF SPIRITS OF THE EARTH
WWW.SPIRITSOFTHEEARTH.COM

▶▶◀◀

It is so very important to me to express my deep gratitude and ayni for all the magical, sacred places and beautiful people I have met on our travels with Shamanic Mystery Tours around the world. I humbly offer a deep bow of gratitude to the beautiful spirits of the Andean people, which also includes our wise shamanic Andean guides and Q'eros *paqos* (shamans). I promise to honor and acknowledge the gifts of their sacred wisdom lineages and initiations—offered through their kind open hearts and generous spirits—by sharing this wisdom with others.

I especially wish to thank my dear Shamanic Sis Star, Vera Lopez, the lead author of this book, whom I feel most fortunate to have met in Sedona many years ago when I answered with an affirmative "Yes!" when she asked if I wanted to travel to Peru to co-lead a 12-12-2012 initiation and opening of the shamanic portals at Machu Picchu. Vera is a living, breathing incarnation of a modern-day shamanic Andean priestess and mystic who remembers prior lifetimes spent in ancient mystery schools at Machu Picchu ages ago. We are quite a contrast on the outside—me with my unruly blond hair, fair skin, and sky-blue eyes and Vera with her raven hair and flashing dark eyes—but beneath our outer appearances we are twin souls who are both passionately committed to the sacred work that we were called to as young women (a few years ago!).

I wish to honor the powerful loving spirit of my late husband, Bradford Clark Collins, who was my work partner for fourteen years with Venus Rising Association for Transformation. We had traveled to Peru before on our own, but our trip to Peru with Vera was extremely powerful and transformative for both of us. Brad experienced a state of illuminated consciousness during the 12-12-12 sunrise ceremony in the shaman's hut at Machu Picchu, which later supported his transition beyond the veils on August 2, 2014.

Also to my father, Richard Finley, whose precious spirit joined Brad on the other side during the writing of this book. I can sense the two of them cheering me on from the other side. Two of the kindest men I have ever known and loved.

Thank you to all kindred spirits everywhere that love and treasure our Earth, Pachamama, and the Great Mystery—and to those who have journeyed with us to this very sacred land and others who will be inspired to make this journey in the future.

Once again with a full heart of gratitude to the incredible publishing team and stellar staff at Inner Traditions • Bear & Company! Thank you, Ehud Sperling, for keeping the vision alive for so many years, which is more important than ever, and to Jeanie Levitan for all that you support. Jamaica Burns Griffin and Manzanita Carpenter Sanz, bless you for your constant dedication to the process!

A very special thank-you to Jon Graham for your continued faith and support in the manuscripts that I have authored, coauthored, or recommended for publication. It means the world to me that Inner Traditions has supported my creations and co-creations of Shamanic Breathwork and Shamanic Mysteries, spreading them all around the world since 2007.

Last but not least, simply from my heart to yours, thank you Nikólaus Wolf for surprising me with the beautiful evolution of our ten-year heart and soul connection. I am so grateful you reminded me that love is all there is and that life and the shamanic spiral path of death and rebirth is eternally full of unexpected surprises when I can just let go of my ego and surrender once again to the Great Mystery and the Spirit of Love.

In sacred ayni and respect for the Shamanic Mysteries of Peru and the Great Mystery,

LINDA STAR WOLF, PH.D.
VENUS RISING ASSOCIATION FOR TRANSFORMATION
WWW.SHAMANICBREATHWORK.ORG

INTRODUCTION

SERPENT OF LIGHT

The Great Shift to the Andes

ANCIENT MYSTICS AND YOGIS TEACH US that the human body has a serpent of energy living within. They refer to this serpent as our kundalini—our life-force energy, our prana, chi, and/or qi. This energy is the force that animates and gives us life. When our kundalini is active and flowing, we experience greater health and vitality. And when our kundalini is blocked we experience dis-ease. Our ancient ancestors knew that when we can uncoil and activate the sleeping serpent living within us—our kundalini life-force energy—we can experience greater levels of spiritual awakening and consciousness.

Just as human beings and animals hold and embody the kundalini serpent, ancient shamans believed that within the core of the Earth resides a Serpent of Light—the energy, force, and spirit that animates all of life on Earth. This Serpent of Light is an activating force for the Earth, and it is believed that this serpent can activate the energy of the culture and traditions of any land where it lays its head.

Drunvalo Melchizedek, author, teacher, and modern-day mystic, shares that the Serpent of Light moves to a new place upon the Earth every thirteen thousand years. Melchizedek teaches that the Serpent of Light began its journey in Lemuria, and then moved to Atlantis, Egypt, India, and Tibet. Throughout its journey, these different cultures were amplified throughout our world and their spiritual traditions were activated within our collective consciousness, or the zeitgeist.

For the past thirteen thousand years, it is believed that the Serpent of Light was situated underneath the Himalayan mountain range. The Himalayan Mountains are home to the world's tallest mountains on the planet. These skyrocketing mountains include Nanga Parbat, Annapurna, Mount Everest, and Kanchenjunga. They spread out over fourteen hundred miles of Asia and surrounding countries, including India, China, and Nepal. Spiritually, these mountains are said to be "Earth altars" or "antennas" of the male polarity, for it is believed that they pull down the masculine energy of the universe and disperse these energies around the globe.

With the Serpent of Light being situated underneath these mountains, our planet Earth experienced thirteen thousand years of life permeated by a strong male vibration. This energetic influence has manifested itself on our planet in a number of ways, including male-focused social structures such as the patriarchy, the widespread indoctrination of belief that there is "one true (male) God," and a heavy focus on capitalism and colonization (the shadow side of the masculine polarity).

In addition to a strong influence of masculine energy, our planet has also experienced a widespread influence of Eastern beliefs and traditions—all primarily emerging from India, China, and Nepal. Practices such as Chinese medicine, meditation, yoga, and breathwork have all been illuminated. These practices have been magnetizing people all around the world—calling them forth to directly experience the wisdom and medicine found within each discipline. All of this amplification and illumination—from the widespread dispersal of masculine energy to the global influence of Eastern beliefs and traditions—is directly related to the positioning of the Serpent of Light underneath the Himalayan mountain range.

On 12-12-12, it is said that the Serpent of Light moved once again, this time from the Himalayan Mountains to the Andes Mountains of South America. Spreading out over thirteen hundred miles, the Andes Mountains can be found in the countries of Venezuela, Chile, Bolivia, Argentina, Colombia, and of course Peru. Much like the Himalayas, the Andes are also believed to be "Earth altars" or "antennas."

The difference between these two mountain ranges is that while the Himalayas channel the masculine polarities onto the Earth, the Andean Mountains pull down and anchor the energies of the feminine polarity.

Since this movement, or great shift, of the Serpent of Light we have seen an increase of awareness around the cultures, practices, and traditions found in South America and its surrounding regions, especially the Peruvian culture.

Today we see more people shifting their diets to include South American foods such as quinoa, acai, cacao, and maca. People from all over the world began to flock to the jungles of South America to experience the medicine of ayahuasca and huachuma (also known as San Pedro)—both of these plant-based hallucinogenic substances can support individuals in shamanic journeys. And in this same movement, thousands of spiritual seekers were called to the ancient sites and temples of Peru and the Incan Empire.

It is no accident that you are reading this book at this moment in time. In fact, we believe that this book is divinely timed and corresponds with the great shift of the ages that is transpiring right now on our planet and within our psyches. The Serpent of Light has awakened the spirits of the Andes, and this serpent is illuminating and bringing forth the shamanic mysteries found in Peru. From the ancient sites of the Incan Empire to the sacred temples and spiritual practices of the Q'eros people—this mystical shamanic wisdom is rising to the surface and coming to light in the hearts and minds of thousands of people all around the world. These practices, traditions, and shamanic mysteries have awakened once again, and they're ready to share their medicine with all those who hear the call.

By picking up this book, you are answering this call . . . Come on the journey with us now, as we lead you to this sacred land. Part 1 of this book delves into the cosmology of Peru, providing an overview for the specifics that are to come. These specifics include an introduction to the Q'eros nation, which is comprised of five communities that in total number two thousand people living at an elevation of approximately sixteen thousand feet in the Andes Mountains. They are the last living descendants of the ancient Inca and, as such, guarded the esoteric wisdom of the community for millennia. In part 1 we also discuss shamanic initiations and sacred symbols that are used in these initiations. Part 2 provides a tour of the sacred land and temples of Peru, including such spiritually revered sites as Cuzco, Moray, Ollantaytambo, Pisac, Machu Picchu, and the Ica region. Part 3 details how best to prepare for an actual or shamanic journey to Peru and includes several illuminating, insightful stories by prior participants. Throughout are meditations and initiations for you to familiarize yourself with Incan cosmology and, at the same time, explore your own inner world.

It's also worth noting that the main narrative of this book is written by Vera Lopez. The sections that are written by Linda Star Wolf are prefaced with headings indicating that this is the case.

So now, take a deep breath and turn the page. In so doing, you begin your journey into the heart and soul of shamanic Peru.

PART 1

▶▶▶ ◀◀◀

THE COSMOLOGY
OF PERU

THE Q'EROS NATION

An Introduction

THROUGHOUT THIS BOOK we will be undergoing a journey through the Andes and we will be receiving the teachings and transmissions found in the Andean Mountains and the shamanic traditions of the people who live there. As you journey through these pages, you will see us using the terms *Andean people* and *Quechua people* interchangeably. When used, each will refer to the small nation of villages located at the high elevations of the Andes Mountains. This nation of villages and the people living within them are known as the Q'eros nation. The traditions, cosmologies, and shamanic wisdom that we will be sharing throughout these pages have been obtained over the past three decades of work directly with the inhabitants of this Andean nation.

ABOUT THE Q'EROS PEOPLE

The Q'eros people have lived for centuries in villages at sixteen thousand feet of elevation. It was thought that these people had disappeared from the Earth, until the year 1950 when they descended from the mountains to share their wisdom and their prophecies with the world. Their history, lore, and traditions, which have been handed down from generation to generation, state that they are of the same lineage as the ancient Mayans, Hopi, Navajo, and Tibetans, and their language and rituals share many similarities.

The people of the Q'eros nation live simple, agricultural lives. They do not have the distractions of our modernized Western world. Due to the high altitude and their dependence upon their farms and crops, the Q'eros people have a deep relationship with the Earth and her elements. They rely on their crops, crafts, and their community to survive the harsh elements of the Andes.

The Q'eros nation is one of the few civilizations on Earth that still holds its ancient teachings and ancient codes intact. Their culture and cosmology are the same as that of their ancient ancestors; their traditions have not been influenced by other cultures.

Quechua, the Language of the Q'eros Nation

The language of the Q'eros people is Quechua. Quechua was the language used in the Incan Empire. Today Quechua is used in the mountain villages scattered throughout Peru, Bolivia, Argentina, and Ecuador. In comparison to the English language, Quechua is a language of few words. One word in Quechua could employ twenty words in English to properly translate and adequately convey the emotion and message it. The Quechua language is based on empathy and emotion; it is a language of transmission and emotional frequency. Behind each word spoken in Quechua there is a depth of meaning and sacred intention.

The Q'eros Symbols and the 5D Codes of Light

Just as the language of the Q'eros people holds deep meaning in each of their words, their symbols and images possess an energetic medicine and timely transmission for our planet. In 2016, filmmakers Eric Heisserer, Ted Chiang, and Denis Villeneuve released the movie *Arrival*—a sci-fi film that portrayed the story of a linguist hired by the American government to translate and decode the language of aliens after twelve mysterious spacecraft landed in different countries throughout the world. In the film, these filmmakers portrayed the alien language as a language of images and symbols—each symbol transmitting an entire code, frequency, and message.

The symbols found in the villages and tribes of the Q'eros people are much like the symbols used by the aliens in the movie. Both the

Q'eros people and the aliens in the movie transmit a powerful download and a code of light in each of their signs and symbols. The Q'eros people are known to be weavers of light, and within each of their crafts and sacred temples they place fifth-dimensional symbols that carry the frequencies of greater love and wisdom. Much like the manner by which one word in the Quechua language possesses so much meaning, one symbol or image can carry a whole download or transmission of knowledge and information from the past and future.

The Shamans: The Paqos

In the Andes Mountains, the medicine men—the shamans—of the Q'eros nation are called *paqos*. *Paqo* is a Quechua word that refers to the priest of the village. In the Andes, the paqos are the lineage carriers of this ancient tradition. These medicine men work with the people to offer healings, blessings, counsel, and initiation. In the Andes, the Q'eros medicine is intentional—any transmissions that you receive from a paqo will be much like an attunement of power. Because this tradition and lineage has been passed down from generation to generation, every time you work with a paqo and receive an initiation—a karpay—from one of these men, you are adopted into their lineage and their ancestors become your ancestors.

GODS AND SPIRITS OF THE Q'EROS PEOPLE

The Q'eros people are a polytheistic culture—they honor many gods. These people also have a strong reverence for their ancestors and for nature. The majority of the gods and deities that we find in Peru are forces of nature that have been personified into a god or deity. This section provides some information about the primary gods, spirits, and deities that we will encounter in our journey throughout Peru.

Viracocha

To the Andes people, Viracocha is the creator of the universe. Viracocha, also known as Huiracocha, Wiraqoca, and Wiro Qocha, is the primary god or godhead within Andean cosmology. He is believed to be the father of all other gods, as well as the creator of the stars, the planets, the Earth, and all of life.

When you journey throughout Peru, you will see statues depicting Viracocha with a serpent, a puma, and a condor. These three animals are sacred to the Andean people, and they hold much gravity in their specific cosmology. To have all three of these animals beside Viracocha communicates to us that Viracocha is the supreme being of the Andean people. With all three of these animal allies, he can journey between the three worlds of the Andes—the Ukhu Pacha, the Kay Pacha, and the Hanan Pacha.

Pachamama

Pachamama is Mother Earth. In the Andes, she is Gaia. Pachamama is the animating force of all life on Earth. She is the soil, the grass, the trees, the animals, the birds. Pachamama is a fertility goddess who bestows blessings upon the Andes people by nurturing the seeds they plant in the ground to grow into healthy and bountiful crops. She is honored and revered within the Q'eros nation, throughout Peru, Bolivia, Argentina, and nowadays all around the world. Pachamama is the nurturing and providing feminine force, the mother of all life.

Mama Killa

Mama Killa is the goddess of the moon. To the Q'eros, Mama Killa is the lunar force that waxes and wanes in the night sky. In the days of the Inca, she provided the knowledge and wisdom of right timing. She influenced the Inca and her insights told them when to plant and harvest, when to move to higher ground, and when to come down the mountain. Mama Killa and her manifestation as the moon greatly influenced the lunar calendar of the Inca. In addition to holding the wisdom of right timing, Mama Killa is also the goddess of a woman's menstrual mysteries, and she supports women as they undergo their monthly flow and cycle.

Inti

Inti is the patron god of the Incan Empire. He is the god of the sun. Inti offers his golden rays of light to Pachamama, who then receives

Inti's light and nourishes the land, allowing crops to grow and flourish. Inti brings light to the darkness—he is the freshness of dawn, the heat of midday, and the gentleness of dusk.

Apus Spirits

In the shamanic traditions of Peru, land spirits are known as Apus spirits. Apus spirits are the spirits of the mountains, the trees, the forest, the jungles, the rivers, the lakes, and the oceans. Each manifestation in nature has an Apus living in it. The mountain of Machu Picchu has an Apus residing within—it is the Apus of Machu Picchu. Huayna Picchu, the mountain behind Machu Picchu, also has an Apus spirit—the Apus of Huayna Picchu. The Urubamba River has an Apus, and the jungles have an Apus. These nature spirits are wise beings of the natural world. They are the great-grandmothers and great-grandfathers of Peru, and when we connect with them we are able to receive much wisdom and guidance from the natural world.

▶▶◀◀

STAR WOLF SPEAKS

THE APUS SPIRIT OF THE LUCUMA TREE

As a little girl growing up in western Kentucky, I had the great fortune and blessing of connecting with nature and the land spirits at an early age. My parents would often send me to my grandmother's house, and it was my grandmother Mammy Jones who always encouraged my relationship with nature. She'd let me sleep with my favorite chickens, and she'd teach me how to plant seeds in the garden—always making sure that I prayed to both Jesus and the fairies so that the seeds would grow into healthy and fruitful plants, flowers, and crops.

I truly loved my Mammy Jones, and to this day I believe she was—and, now from the other side, continues to be—one of my greatest shamanic teachers. When I was twelve years old and she died suddenly, my world was shattered. I felt as if the only person in the world who truly understood and saw me had left the planet. My grandmother's death was one of my earliest shamanic initiations, and this heartbreaking experience catapulted me into my destiny . . .

As I reflect back on one of my first journeys to Peru, I can see why I instantly felt at home and fell in love with the Sacred Valley, which is often referred to as a place of nurturing and healing especially for the heart and spirit. The ancient cascading Andes Mountains stand as elders and guardians in its backdrop and provide a sense of protection and safety. I had a most profound connection with one of its oldest residents, a one-thousand-year-old sacred Lucuma tree, which grows in a friend's garden in the Sacred Valley. In Peru, Lucuma trees are sacred to the Andes people, for they believe that these trees possess special healing powers, and they've been found planted along the burial sites of the ancient people. Lucuma trees have a long and healthy lifespan. They are native to the valleys of Peru and Ecuador and are able to grow to a height of sixty-five feet. Upon meeting this wise old soul, I felt an immediate connection with the Lucuma tree and promised myself, and her, that I would return whenever I could to connect with her.

Although I visited with her upon several occasions, one day stands out as a very special transmission between the two of us. On this particular day that I paid Grandmother Lucuma a visit, I was already in an altered state of consciousness—the state of consciousness one naturally obtains when doing Shamanic Breathwork in high altitudes and just by being barefoot in nature.

As I approached the tree, I could feel her immense wisdom. This Lucuma tree was approximately sixty feet tall, and when I was standing within her presence, I could feel her and her energy encapsulate me. To reach this height above ground meant that her roots were equally long. As I stood at her base, I imagined the intricate system supporting her from below—spreading down and out, grabbing onto the rocks in the Earth, intertwining with the other trees and plants in the garden and drawing up different nutrients and minerals to support this wise grandmother. I sat down at her base and wrapped my legs and arms around her. While I couldn't fully embrace her, as she was much larger than my physical body, I sat with her and leaned my face and body against her bark and allowed her to hold me.

As I sat with her, I imagined all of the many seasons she had witnessed. I envisioned all of the different ceremonies and events this Lucuma tree had been part of, knowing that she had stood as a sacred guardian on this land for over a thousand years—witnessing the rise and fall of many societies and civilizations. I held her and breathed into this vision, and as I reflected on all that she had witnessed and all that she had experienced, I was reminded that change is the only constant in life. All life must change and, in so doing, enter into the shamanic process of life, death, and rebirth.

As I held her and she held me I could feel her reassure me much like a grandmother would a small grandchild. Being held within her presence, I could feel, trust, and know that whatever was unfolding in my world—whatever challenges and obstacles I was destined to face—I was going to be okay. She reassured me that I was just like her—strong and resilient. And even though my roots early in life had been fragile, they had supported me in finding the shamanic world in the midst of nature, and through this discovery I was able to strengthen my roots with each passing day.

The Lucuma tree understood my longing for my Mammy Jones, and she could feel my desire for a connection with my grandmother's elders. As she held me, she energetically conveyed to me that all I had to do was come to her or some other place in nature, and connect with the energy of the wise grandmothers there. She conveyed to me that this can be done anywhere in nature, and that these wise elder spirits were my grandparents and that they would be willing to support me in anything.

As I sat there and received this download, I suddenly felt as if my Mammy Jones were speaking directly to me through this tree. I could feel her hold me, and I could feel her comfort the little girl in me who felt that she had to be strong for everyone in the world. This experience left a profound impact on my life, as I was able to embody the knowing that this little girl within me didn't need to be strong anymore. She had everything she needed and she could allow herself to be held by a force larger than her. I realized later on that I had experienced a deep healing and soul retrieval with the lost parts of the little girl that had exited when my own grandmother had passed away so many years before.

I bowed as I stood up and gave thanks to this wise being for holding me and sharing much wisdom with me, I felt an inner calling to offer her my favorite silver bracelet. My bracelet was a simple one that had the words *serenity* and *surrender* engraved on it. This bracelet was a talisman of mine—I never took it off. I slept with it, showered with it, and I'd worn it for so long that it left a scar on my arm. It was a symbol of my ongoing sobriety and my daily commitment to follow my truth each and every day. I knew in that moment that I had received so much wisdom and soul healing from this amazing tree and I wanted to reciprocate what I had been freely given.

So I took off the bracelet, kissed it, held it to my heart, and imparted a blessing of gratitude. I noticed a small crevice in the bark of the tree, and I gently pushed my bracelet into it. When I did this, something opened up in the tree and took my bracelet. I knew that the Lucuma tree had received my gift. To this day, I still feel our strong bond and heart connection, and I am forever grateful for the medicine she imparted to me on this sacred day.

The teachings and traditions of the Q'eros people are simple yet deeply profound. In the Andes, you will not find high ceremonies or complicated systems of thought and belief. For the Andes people, life is about the reciprocity in relationships—our relationship with the Pachamama (the Earth), the Apus spirits, the sun, the moon, the stars, and our relationship with each other. Their teachings and traditions are inherently based upon this philosophy of reciprocity and the understanding (and awareness) that we are all connected. What happens to one person happens to us all.

AYNI

The Law of Reciprocity

If we were meant to live life alone, Creator would have only made one of us.

GRANDMOTHER TWYLAH

In the traditions of Andean shamanism, the Andes people view the world as an interconnected being of existence. They believe that everything is connected to one another and supports the existence of one another—the mineral kingdom supports the plant kingdom, and the plant kingdom supports the animal kingdom. The people of the Andes, and especially those who honor the ancient ways of their shamanic ancestors, walk through life with the viewpoint that all of life is sacred; everything within the cosmos resides within a governing principle of reciprocity. To the Q'eros people, this governing principle of reciprocity is known as the law of ayni.

In Quechua, *ayni* means "today for you, tomorrow for me." Ayni is the primary law of the Andean people. It is the principle of reciprocity that maintains balance for them in their lives, their communities, and all of their relations upon the Earth. In the Andes, and especially in the high regions and elevations of the Q'eros nation, nothing is given without something being received, and nothing is received without something else being given in exchange. This is a cycle of energy that the Andes people honor and revere; for them, ayni is law. They believe that we are always in this cycle of giving and receiving—we are always in the flow of ayni.

When I look back and remember my very first journeys to Peru over thirty years ago, I can remember the weather being frigid. I would look out at the mountains, and the mountain caps would be covered with snow. It was a beautiful sight, and it was cold. During these first journeys to Peru, my groups and I would bundle up in our warm winter coats and jackets and walk around the city of Cuzco at night. As we made our way through the streets, looking at the moon and the stars, we would always stumble upon several Andean children late at night.

"What are you doing on the streets at this hour?" I would ask the children. "It is late, and you should be at home, warm in your beds."

"We are hungry. We haven't eaten all day. Do you have some bread?" the children asked us with hungry eyes.

Of course, none of us had any snacks or food on us, so I took it upon myself to find a restaurant that was still open, and purchased several loaves of bread for these children. When I brought it back to them, you would have thought they would have immediately eaten it, but they did not. Instead, they broke the loaves into several pieces and found their friends and siblings (who were also out roaming the streets, searching for food) and shared their bread with them.

These children never asked us for money, they only asked us for food. Upon receiving the bread, the children offered me a bracelet in return.

"No, you do not need to give me anything," I told them. After all, I was thinking that they could sell the bracelet in the market and make money for themselves and their families.

However, they insisted that I take it as an exchange for the bread, and so I did. At the time I was unaware that this was my first experience with ayni.

As I continued my journeys to Peru, I discovered the immense level of poverty within its different villages and cities. Seeing the number of children and families living without enough warm clothing, shoes, and food, I began to take large amounts of blankets and jackets with me each time I journeyed to Peru. During each trip, I would make a point to walk around the cities and hand out these jackets and blankets to all the children that I found roaming the streets. Each time I gifted one of them with a blanket or a jacket, they would always find something to give me in return, whether it was a stone, a small piece of pottery, a poppet, or something else that they had made.

My practice of giving grew, and I began visiting the local villages tucked away in the high mountains. I would bring suitcases full of blankets, jackets, shoes, and food and share it with these people. Once again, I would find them offering me gifts in exchange. In the beginning, I found this practice of theirs strange—these people barely had enough food for themselves and their families yet here they were gifting me with a potato or a craft that they made to sell in the market.

As time went on I discovered that if I did not receive their gifts and exchanges, I would be breaking the cycle of energy that they honor and revere, because in ayni there is no such thing as "one-sided giving." Again, in ayni, we all receive every time we give, and we give every time we receive. Through this practice, the cycle of energy continues to flow—maintaining the balance in our lives and in our relationships. (In terms of this practice of giving and receiving, over time it grew, until finally it evolved into an organization that is known as the Ayni Project, which you can read more about in the appendix to this book.)

Although in comparison to our Westernized world, it may appear that this practice of ayni and the other teachings of the people of the Andes are "simple," the Andean cosmology has been passed down from generation to generation. There is timelessness to this culture as their beliefs have not been diluted by outside influence; their ways of living and engaging with the natural and spiritual worlds still carry the authentic medicine and wisdom of their advanced ancestors and their ancient lineage.

I truly believe that the Q'eros people and the traditions of Peru have deep medicine for our modern world, which today is filled with distractions, anxiety, and depression. Our modernized world has been disconnected from the natural world and we are experiencing a soul loss from our shamanic roots. I believe that the medicine and wisdom found in the Andes Mountains can remind us to slow down, take a deep breath, and remember that we are truly connected to everyone and everything. I trust that when we are able to remember this connection—to each other and to the natural world—we will be like the hummingbird and embody the joy that is inherent in our being and in our existence.

CHAKANA

Symbol of Andean Cosmology

THROUGH DIFFERENT CULTURES, religions, and spiritual traditions, we see humans make sense of the world around them by creating codes of spiritual practices and beliefs. These practices and beliefs are usually derived from the natural world. In ancient indigenous cultures we see the personification of the elements of earth, air, fire, and water; we see animals representing different spiritual attributes and supernatural abilities. Our ancient shamanic ancestors drew upon the forces of the natural world and used these forces to gain understanding of the universe. Through the synthesis of these elements and their observations gleaned from the natural world, our ancestors created systems of beliefs. These systems of beliefs are known today as cosmologies.

Cosmologies include and shed light on:

* the cultural understandings of divinity
* the pathways of life and consciousness
* the realms of consciousness
* principles carried out and embodied in the cultural lifestyle

When we look into the traditions of the Andes, we find a symbol that communicates the entirety of the Andean cosmology. This symbol is the Chakana. In today's modern world, many people refer to the Chakana as the Incan cross, equating this symbol to that of the

Christian cross, which is not accurate. The ancient Andean people did not have the early influence of the Judeo-Christian belief system, so they did not recognize the cross as one of their sacred symbols. Nor did they share the same understanding of the cross that modern-day Christian believers have.

The word *Chakana* stems from the Quechua word *chakay*, which means "to bridge" or "to cross." To the ancient Andean people, the Chakana was the sacred geometry of the Inca. Within its geometric shapes resides an energetic code—a transmission that shared how the shamans of the Andes view the universe and all the relationships within the cosmos. To the Andes people, the Chakana symbolically represents

Chakana with animal totems Puma, Serpent, and Condor

their principles and values, and illustrates all the facets of the Andean cosmology.

DECODING THE CHAKANA

When we look at the Chakana we see a four-pointed cross with a series of three ridges in between each cross point. Within this geometric design, we see a square, a circle, and a triangle, and within the center of the Chakana there is a round circle opening.

The Tawantinsuyus

The outer four points of the cross represent the *tawantinsuyus*—the four empires of the Incan Empire. At its greatest peak of power, the Incan Empire joined Peru, the southwest region of Ecuador, western and central portions of Bolivia, the northwest region of Argentina, northern Chile, and a small portion of Colombia. This vast region of land dominated by the Inca was known as Tawantinsuyu—the Empire of the Four Directions. Each of the four cardinal directions—North, East, South, and West—housed a specific empire within the larger Incan Empire. The four empires were:

 * Chinchaysuyu, Empire of the North
 * Qullasuyu, Empire of the South
 * Antisuyu, Empire of the East
 * Quntisuyu, Empire of the West

These four empires, or *suyus,* extended from the city of Cuzco, which was the capital city of the Incan Empire, and together covered about 770,000 square miles of land in South America. The four outer points of the Chakana are symbolic of these four empires, the tawantinsuyus, and they represent the vast reach of the Incan Empire.

The Three Worlds within the Chakana

The square, the circle, and the triangle within the Chakana each represent a dimension or world within the Andean cosmology. Within each of these worlds stands a guardian, or totem—an animal that spiritually and symbolically carries, embodies, and protects these worlds and the wisdom they hold within. In the shamanic traditions of North America, the indigenous people placed totems in each of the four directions of the medicine wheel. In the Andes, the shamans place their power animals in the three worlds of their cosmology.

The three worlds of the Andean cosmology and their animal totems are:

* The Ukhu Pacha: the lower world guarded by the serpent
* The Kay Pacha: the middle world guarded by the puma
* The Hanan Pacha: the upper world guarded by the condor

The square of the Chakana symbolizes the Hanan Pacha. The triangle represents the Ukhu Pacha, and the circle represents the Kay Pacha. These three worlds and their animal guardians are the framework of the universe for the shamans of Peru. Within each of these worlds and dimensions we can journey and find different mysteries and wisdom teachings.

The Teachings and Principles of the Chakana

In between each of the four main points of the Chakana—in between the points that represent the Empires of the Four Directions—we see three ridges, or steps. Within the entire Chakana we see a total of twelve steps. Each of these steps represents a concept and/or principle that was deeply valued in the Incan Empire and is still honored and revered by the Quechua people today.

Beginning on the upper point of the Chakana, the North point, and making our way to the right to the East point, these three steps represent:

* Present
* Productivity
* Responsibility

The steps going from the East to the South, the lower point on the Chakana, represent:

+ Expression
+ Passion
+ Happiness

From South to West, the left point on the Chakana, these steps symbolize the principles of:

+ Awareness
+ Protection
+ Acknowledgment

Moving from the West point back to the North point, we see these steps carrying the frequency of:

+ Connections
+ Trust
+ Love

Each of these twelve concepts are key to the Andean lifestyle. The Andean people believe that living in balance and in relationship to each of these principles brings joy and wholeness to one's life.

The Center of the Chakana

The center of the Chakana represents and symbolizes Cuzco—the capital city of the Incan Empire. For the early Inca, Cuzco was the center of their empire. Its name stems from the Quechua word *qosqo,* which translates to "center" or "navel." To the Incan and Andean people, Cuzco is believed to be the "Navel of the Earth." The city of Cuzco is held in high esteem in modern-day Peruvian culture, for it still carries the same magnetism and mysticism that it did at the time of the early Inca.

Traditionally the center of the Chakana is left open. This opening is believed to create a portal—a doorway to the various dimensions and worlds of the Andean cosmology. When we work with this rich symbol in meditation or use it in shamanic journeys, we can use this center portal to enter the Ukhu Pacha, the Kay Pacha, and/or the Hanan Pacha. Using the center we can also journey to and connect with the twelve different principles found around the Chakana, and we can work with these energies to bring balance and wholeness to our lives.

As mentioned before, the people of the Andes are people of intention. Each of their words has deep meaning, and each symbol holds a transmission. When we look at the different symbolic meanings of the Chakana we are able to see an example of these ancient people using symbolic codes and sacred geometry to share and transmit their traditions and their cosmology.

THE THREE WORLDS OF THE ANDEAN COSMOLOGY

You've always had the power, my dear. You just had to learn it for yourself.
GLINDA, THE GOOD WITCH, *THE WIZARD OF OZ*

In shamanic traditions all around the world, we understand the shamanic perspective that the universe is separated into three different levels of existence—an upper world, a middle world, and a lower world. If we were to look at a tree, figuratively as a metaphor for these three worlds of existence, we would see the roots of the tree as a symbol of the lower world, the trunk of the tree symbolizing the middle world, and the branches of the tree as a symbolic representation of the upper world.

Each of these worlds contain different elements, creatures, and spirits specific to the shamanic traditions found in different regions of the world. In each shamanic culture and society, the role of the shaman is to walk between these different worlds of existence, connect with the spirits and energies that reside there, and bring the multidimensional wisdom and medicine that they find there back to their tribes and communities.

In the shamanic tradition of the Andes, the shamans believe that the universe is composed of three different pachas. *Pacha* is the Quechua word for "earth" or "world." Again, the three pachas of the Andean cosmology are:

- The Ukhu Pacha: the lower world
- The Kay Pacha: the middle world
- The Hanan Pacha: the upper world

Each of these worlds is its own distinct dimension, and each holds a special wisdom and medicine. Shamans view each of these pachas as an actual place of existence where they can journey to find vision, connect with ancestors, study universal principles, reclaim lost soul parts, and receive great healing, wisdom, and transformation.

While each of these worlds can be viewed as an actual dimensional place of existence, from a modern shamanic psycho-spiritual perspective, they can also be seen as representations of certain aspects of our psyche and consciousness. For example, the Ukhu Pacha can represent our unconscious mind, or shadow self; the Kay Pacha can represent our conscious mind; and the Hanan Pacha can represent our soul, or highest self. Each and every day we can make it a part of our shamanic practice to check in with these different worlds living within us. We can take a shamanic journey to see how the elements of these worlds are influencing our everyday life. We can find guidance from the spirits that reside in these three pachas, and when these three worlds are aligned and balanced in ourselves we can experience an integrated and healthy life.

THE UKHU PACHA

The Snake within the Andean Underworld

No tree, it is said, can grow to heaven unless its roots reach down to hell.

CARL JUNG, SWISS PSYCHOLOGIST

To the Andean people, the Ukhu Pacha is the lower world. In Quechua, *Ukhu* translates to "what is in." Andean shamans believed that everything inside, literally within the core of the Earth, as well as below the Earth was held in the domain of the Ukhu Pacha. The Ukhu Pacha is the Andean underworld; it is their valley of shadows, or shadow world.

Due to some of these representations, many people confuse and compare the Ukhu Pacha with the Judeo-Christian notion of "hell," and this could not be further from the truth. To the Andean people, there is no need to sanction a space for eternal damnation or punishment, for all of life is sacred, and all of life is connected. In fact, the Andean people believe that when they bury their dead ones in the Earth, they are actually placing them into the Ukhu Pacha—a sacred land in which the dead may rest and restore their spirits.

In the Andes, the Quechua people believe that the caves and springs in the mountains are the doorways, or bridges, to the Ukhu Pacha, as the Ukhu Pacha rests just beneath the surface of our physical world and reality.

When we journey to the realms of the Ukhu Pacha we can experience great levels of healing and discover which aspects of ourselves need more time to mature and develop. Here in the Ukhu Pacha, we can work with our shadow self—the unclaimed aspects of our psyche and being. Throughout our journey and our work here in the lower world, we can find acceptance for these pieces of ourselves and integrate them back into our being. In shamanic psycho-spiritual practices, this is the art of soul retrieval—bringing lost soul parts, or pieces of ourselves, back into our bodies, hearts, and spirits.

The triangle in the Chakana carries the code of the Ukhu Pacha and it represents the Great Serpent that resides within this underground world.

The Great Serpent

When we look at the medicine and wisdom of the snake we can learn more about the dimension of the Ukhu Pacha. In all cultures across the world, snakes represent wisdom, transformation, healing, and spiritual awakening. In the Bible, the snake came down from the tree and tempted Eve with the fruit of knowledge. The Egyptians had a cobra-snake goddess named Wadjet, and she was believed to be the great awakener of our kundalini life-force energy. In our modern-day world, the medical profession is represented by the ancient Greek symbol known as the caduceus, which is the staff of Hermes. It's depicted as a rod that is crowned with a pair of wings and has two snakes winding up its staff. Throughout time and millennia, shamanic traditions across the world (and those of the Quechua people are no exception) have revered the snake for its transformative medicine of healing, primal life-force energy, spiritual awakening, death, and rebirth.

To the Quechua people and their ancient shamanic ancestors, the Great Serpent was the guardian of the Ukhu Pacha. To them, Mother Snake was a guide for healing, renewal, and rebirth. Every time the Andes people witness a snake shedding its skin, they know that Mother Snake is undergoing her own process of death and rebirth.

They understood and viewed this shedding process—this letting go of the old form and the old self—as an initiation within the Ukhu Pacha. Watching Mother Snake shed her skin, they would witness and observe her eyes cloud over, hindering her sense of sight and making her vulnerable to predators. They understood that when they came across a snake in this part of the process, the spirit of this snake was deep within the underworld journey, visioning for a new skin—a new form, and a new sense of self. As they watched Mother Snake surrender and let go of her old skins, they simultaneously witnessed her death and her rebirth.

As she emerges from the underworld, releasing her old skin, Mother Snake emerges from her death and comes back to life with a renewed beauty. Her skin is shiny and new, her energy is awakened and restored, and all the old aspects of her that weighed her down and tightened her up have been shed away.

When we journey to the Ukhu Pacha we have the opportunity to work with Mother Snake. Deep within the darkness of the lower world we can discover what aspects of ourselves are no longer working. We can feel into our bodies and see where we need to make a change. Mother Snake can guide us in releasing all the aspects of our lives that weigh us down and keep us stuck. Whether you have an illness or a dis-ease of a physical, mental, emotional, or spiritual nature, Mother Snake can guide you through the portals of transformation and healing. During our journey through the Ukhu Pacha, we can let go of all of our old ego identities, our old ways of being, and surrender them to Mother Snake, so that we may experience rebirth and renewal.

Mother Snake can guide you through the shadows of the Ukhu Pacha and support you as you let go of your old sense of self and are reborn into your new way of being.

SHAMANIC JOURNEY
TO THE UKHU PACHA
Guided by Vera Lopez

Take a deep breath and exhale fully. Close your eyes and take another deep breath. Feel your body expand with each inhale and feel your body contract with each exhale. The time has come for you to begin your journey—a journey that will initiate you and accelerate you on your path to wholeness and transformation . . .

As you breathe deeply, imagine yourself walking along a path through the Andes Mountains of Peru. The path winds through the mountains. It curves around the trees and takes you around large boulders and stones that are from a time not too distant from our own. Below you can see the great Urubamba River snaking its way through the valley of mountains. You look up and notice that it's dusk—the sun is setting. As you take in the wonder of sunset in the Andes, you notice a condor swoop down from a mountain peak and fly off into the light of the setting sun.

As you continue your journey along the path, you discover the mouth of a cave up ahead. You journey to the cave and make your way inside, where it is dark and cold yet not uncomfortable. You walk further into it and discover that there is a spiraling staircase leading further down. You step onto the staircase and begin your spiral descent down into the heart of the cave.

As you journey down the staircase you notice that the temperature in the cave begins to get warmer, and you can see the growing flickering of light down below. As you get closer and descend down into the cave further, you reach a level plateau and an opening. Stepping off the staircase you walk into the opening, where you see a giant, blazing fire. The flames of this fire snake their way throughout the heart of the cave, illuminating the area around you.

You walk closer to the fire and feel its warmth. As you stand looking into it, you notice some movement on the other side of the flames. As you look closer you realize that the movement is a huge snake—the Great Serpent of the Ukhu Pacha. This snake uncoils itself and moves around the fire. It positions itself in front of you and then rises, meeting you at eye level.

As you and the Great Serpent stare into each other's eyes, you begin to feel a shift occurring within you and you realize that you are able to journey into your own heart and soul. You are able to see and examine all of the areas in your life that you've outgrown. These can be relationships, behaviors, careers, thought patterns, or some other form of your old ego identity. As you breathe and continue to journey with this serpent, you begin to bring these old ego identities to the surface of your consciousness and you begin to let them go.

One by one you allow these different pieces of who you used to be to leave your body, mind, and spirit. The old ego identities leave your field and solidify on the ground in between you and the Great Serpent. After you've released these different ego parts and pieces from your body, mind, and spirit, the Great Serpent lowers itself down to your old ego identity. It opens its mouth and it swallows all that is no longer who you truly are. The Great Serpent swallows all the pain from your past, all the heartache, sadness, and grief. It swallows all of the limitations of who you once were and frees you to become the person you were born to be.

Watching the snake swallow your old ego whole, you begin to feel a sense of relief, freedom, and liberation. There is a lightness to your field and you feel expanded after releasing all that no longer serves you. You move and stretch, allowing this feeling of lightness and freedom to expand throughout your body.

You turn to face the snake, who is once again at eye level with you, and you offer gratitude to this wise, ancient being. You give thanks to this being who knows how to change and transform, how to shed and release the old and begin again. You give thanks to this being, as it has helped you in your own process of transformation. You give the serpent an offering of your own hair or a blessing from your heart. The serpent flicks its tongue and receives your blessing and offering of gratitude and slides away, back to its home behind the fire where it will transmute your old identities into a new form.

You take in the warmth of the fire once again and you look around the cave once more. This has been your journey and experience in the Ukhu Pacha. You take some time to anchor this memory and this experience into your heart and into your body. You bow to the energies of the Great Below and find your way back to the staircase.

As you begin your climb—your ascent from the underworld—you notice that you are beginning to feel more connected to your body and your breath. You breathe in and you feel the strength that has come with the shedding of your old ego. You continue to feel light and expanded as you climb up the spiral staircase back into the Kay Pacha. Your sense of vision and purpose, and your connection to your human needs and drives, are heightened. You know with clarity what you need, what you want, and what you desire.

You reach the top of the staircase and see the opening of the cave door that called you to initiate your journey. It is now nighttime. The stars are out and they are shining down upon you from the Great Above.

You find the winding path and follow it back to your body, back into your time and space, back into your physical dimension. Breathe in and breathe out. Wiggle your fingers and toes and allow yourself to return.

THE HANAN PACHA

The Condor and the Upper World

High above the mountain peaks, hidden behind the mists, resides the unseen world of the Hanan Pacha—the upper world of the Andean cosmology. To the Andean people, the Hanan Pacha is the realm, or "earth," of the heavens. Within the realm of Hanan Pacha resides the sun, the moon, the stars, and all things that live above and outside of the Earth. This is the place of the Great Above, and it is the home of Great Mystery, God/dess, and the I AM presence. The Hanan Pacha is the home of the gods.

Because this dimension resides outside the Earth and physical reality, and because it is believed to be the realm of the gods, Hanan Pacha holds a deep source of wisdom and knowledge. When we journey to the Hanan Pacha, we can access this great spiritual wisdom and use it to enrich our lives, the lives of our families, and the lives of all those within our tribes and communities. The Hanan Pacha is the place we journey to pray and to commune with the gods, and to receive wisdom from the unseen world.

Journeying to the Hanan Pacha, we are able to see life's bigger picture. Much like the journey made in climbing a tall mountain, sometimes in life we are unable to recognize how every step and every experience along the way supports us and enhances our journey. When we reach the top of the mountain, and we are able to look out and take in the vastness of the view before us, we are able to understand that everything in our life—every action, relationship, experience—has a sacred purpose and contributes to our soul and its journey. This state of awareness and level of consciousness is Hanan Pacha—from this place we can see all of life through the eyes of the gods.

The Condor

The Guardian of the Hanan Pacha is Condor.

Similar to the eagle in the North American shamanic traditions, the condor embodies a majesty and regality to the Andes people. Having a wingspan that reaches anywhere between eight to ten feet, and being known as the highest-flying bird in South America, it is no wonder that the condor is associated with the Hanan Pacha, the realm of the gods.

Because the Andes people witnessed the condor flying to great heights in the skies and swiftly disappearing in the mists of the tallest mountains, they believed that it was the only creature that could journey between this world and the world of the gods, the Hanan Pacha. They believed that each sight or visit from the condor was a direct message from the gods of the Great Above, and with each sighting they believed they had received a blessing from the Hanan Pacha.

While condors are known to deliver messages from the gods to the Andes people, condors are also able to carry the prayers of the Q'eros paqos to the gods. Because of this, condor feathers are highly valued tools for shamans, as these feathers are believed to hold a direct connection to gods of the universe and the Hanan Pacha. Using these feathers while praying or in ceremony is believed to deliver one's prayers and intentions directly to the ears of the gods above.

The ancients held great reverence for their winged relatives, for they knew that these creatures frequently visited with the Divine and they had access to otherworldly knowledge and wisdom.

SHAMANIC JOURNEY

TO THE HANAN PACHA
Guided by Vera Lopez

Take a deep breath and exhale fully. Close your eyes and breathe deeply into your lungs, filling your body with oxygen and chi. Take a deep breath in and exhale completely. Lie down and allow yourself to get comfortable.

In your mind's eye, envision yourself high up in the Andes Mountains, sitting on a rock ledge that has been there for millennia. Looking out in front of you, you can see an ocean of mountains extending as far as your eyes can see. Carefully looking down below, you can make out the Urubamba River moving through the base of these mountains. From high up this ancient powerful river snakes through the mountains, looking like a silver snake winding its way through the Andes jungle. Above you, mists and clouds gently descend down from the skies above.

As you breathe and take in the surroundings on this high mountain ledge, you notice a condor flying off in the distance. You watch this majestic bird fly through the clouds and mountaintops, gliding through the currents of the wind. Moving with such grace and ease, you notice that the condor is getting closer and closer to your ledge. You stand up and it flies in closer and lands on your ledge. You and the condor exchange glances. Looking deep into its eyes, you feel and know that you are in the presence of a divine being.

This condor is large. Spreading out its wings, you realize that this condor is large enough to hold and carry you—a mythical creature from the otherworld.

The condor turns to the edge of the ledge, facing the ocean of mountains. The condor turns back to look at you and welcomes you to jump on its back. You approach and climb upon the giant condor and once you are settled and comfortable the condor leaps off the ledge and flies into the mists and into the ocean of mountains.

Flying high above the mountains and soaring through the mists, Condor shows you the portals and doorways to the hidden realms of the Great Above—the Hanan Pacha. Condor takes you to the first doorway, the doorway of your past. You and Condor both fly through the portal and enter a scene from your past—perhaps this is a memory or experience from your childhood, or a series of events from a past life. Take note of where you are, what you are experiencing, what you are witnessing. Are there any feelings associated with this past memory? Take some time to drop into this past experience . . .

After you've allowed yourself to revisit this past experience, see if there is any medicine that wishes to come back with you from it. Perhaps there is a symbol, a color, a message—whatever wants to come back with you, do not judge it; just allow it to come back for further integration. Thank this portal to the past. Soon you climb upon the condor once again.

Condor lifts off and together you fly through the portal to the past and enter back into the in-between worlds. Condor flies further and you can feel how it uses the current of the wind to support its flight and direction. Gliding forward, Condor flies into the portal to the present. Flying through the portal, you and Condor land in a present time and memory in your life. Take note of where you are. What time in the present are you in? Where are you—does this location have a certain scenery, a certain feeling? Take note and see if there are any other people in this present-memory experience. Do you recognize anyone? Take some time to observe and witness what is occurring in your portal to the present.

After allowing yourself some time in the present, see if there is any medicine that wishes to come back with you. Perhaps there is a sign, a symbol, an emotion, a resolution, or a new perspective that wishes to come back with you. Whatever it is, do not judge your medicine but welcome it forward and place it in the medicine chest of your heart for further integration.

Give thanks to this experience from the present, and connect once again with Condor. Once you climb upon its back, Condor flies once again into the air, leaving the portal of the present behind.

Flying through the portal and into the time and space between worlds, Condor soars steadily with the current and flies steadily into the portal of the future. There is no space for the condor to land or perch, so the two of you continue to soar above all the events that are to come in your lifetime. You look down upon these events and see them in the landscape below the condor as it flies.

Take note of what experiences, what outcomes, and what medicine is available to you in the future realms. Breathe into the limitlessness of your future existence and feel the expansiveness of your future lifetime. As you soar through the future, take some time to connect with the messages that your future self has to share. Are there solutions or resolutions available to you from a future perspective? Does your future self have medicine for you? Breathe into the wisdom from your future self and feel this medicine permeate your field.

The condor swoops down and around a mountain and flies back to the portal, to the in-between worlds. The condor catches the current back to the portal to the ledge where your journey began. The condor flies back through the Andes Mountains and the mists. You see the Urubamba River snaking its way through the mountains and the jungle. The condor lands upon the ledge, nestled high above in the mountaintops. You step off the condor and land back on the ledge.

You sit down and begin to pull out the pieces of medicine you acquired from your past, present, and future timelines. The condor spreads its wings and holds space for you as you examine the symbols, experiences, and medicine from these three timelines. Take some time to reflect on everything that you've acquired from this experience. Remember your past, your present, and your future. Breathe into each of these and allow the wisdom from each of these journeys to anchor within you.

Thank the condor for its support and guidance on this multidimensional journey. Breathe back into your body. Wiggle your fingers and toes. And when you are ready, open your eyes.

THE KAY PACHA

Puma and the Middle World

As above, so below. As within, so without.

ANCIENT SPIRITUAL MAXIM

In between the Ukhu Pacha and the Hanan Pacha resides our world, the middle world of the Andean cosmology—the Kay Pacha. The Kay Pacha is our physical reality. It is our dimension of consciousness. The circle within the Chakana represents the Kay Pacha and all the mysteries that live in this realm of existence and consciousness.

To the Andean people, the Kay Pacha holds the domain for the life that we live and experience; it is life on Earth. Everything that you see in this world—the trees, the rivers, the oceans, the animals, the plants—everything on Earth resides in the Kay Pacha.

While the Ukhu Pacha is the world of the dead, and the Hanan Pacha is the realm of the gods, the Kay Pacha is the world of life and the living. Within the Kay Pacha we can embody our physical bodies and live our soul's purpose. It is in this dimension that we can experience all of the mysteries of life. In this realm we can experience love, connection, joy, ecstasy, sorrow, and bliss.

The Kay Pacha is a dimension of experience and integration. From this world we can journey to the Ukhu Pacha and the underworld, and we can soar with Condor to the greatest heights of the Hanan Pacha. However, regardless of which dimension we journey to, we must always come back to this physical reality to integrate and ground the medicine we've received from these other dimensions. The Kay Pacha is the world where we merge the wisdom of the Above with the wisdom found in the Below.

Being that the Kay Pacha is the integration of the Great Above and the Great Below, Kay Pacha also represents and holds the frequency of the Great Within. The Great Within is where we can find the essence of our truest self, our authentic self. Our Great Within is the fusion of our highest self, residing in the Great Above, and our shadow self, residing in the Great Below. Here within the Kay

Pacha—or the Great Within—we can journey to find the wisdom of our heart. We can connect with what we value, love, and desire, and we can channel these energies from the Great Within into our everyday life.

The Puma

The guardian of the Kay Pacha is Puma.

Living in the Kay Pacha we must be strong, active, and find ways to survive all of life's initiations. This dimension requires us to take action, to be warriors, and to fully embody our physical strength and vitality.

Puma is the guardian and guide of the Kay Pacha, because to the Andes people the puma is the warrior of the animal kingdom. Puma knows how to survive in all of the elements and all the seasons. It knows how to hunt—discerning when to stalk its prey and when to take action to live.

Puma can teach us how to witness and observe our fears and still move forward. Puma can grant us the energy to move beyond the limitations of our mind and embody the vitality of the heart. It can teach us the wisdom of life and allow us to see the interconnectedness of every plant, mineral, and creature on our planet, and it can guide us to live in harmony with all of life.

Puma Medicine in the "Heart" of Peru
Stephanie Red Feather

Chatting happily with one of my travel mates, I suddenly stopped talking and proclaimed with glazed eyes, "I'm feeling a bit woozy and lightheaded. I need to breathe and try to ground myself." A couple of minutes later our bus pulled into the parking lot of our destination.

We departed the bus and our guide, Vera, chose for us to traverse a short tunnel through a rock outcropping to enter into the belly of this particular sacred site. She told us that the center of the passageway would be completely dark, so we should carefully slide our hands along the walls to keep our bearing.

I was already altered, but as we walked toward the hole in the rock, the tears began. As I stepped into the tunnel, my body started shaking with uncontrollable sobs. Entering the pitch-black section deliberately, I wasn't in a hurry to get back to the light on the other side. In fact, I wanted to stay there and lay my entire body against the wall and collapse into Mother Earth. I did this for a brief moment, sensitive to the people following not far behind me.

When I emerged from the tunnel, it was as if a time warp had occurred. I was completely out of my body and could barely manage to shuffle my feet. Sacsayhuamán had a hold on me and I had no choice but to surrender to her spell.

Sacsayhuamán (we were encouraged to think "sexy woman" to remember it) is a sacred site outside of Cuzco, Peru, which I had the privilege of visiting for the first time in October 2018. Later that day when I asked Vera a bit more about its meaning and configuration, she said Sacsayhuamán was designed to be the head of the puma (even sporting a zigzag wall intended to represent the puma's teeth) while Cuzco, adjacent to the site, was meant to be the puma's body.

Of course it was.

When I embark on a spiritual journey or travel to sacred sites, I am very conscious not to have an expectation, yet I am always aware that magic awaits. What was awaiting me in Peru was a personal animal guide who would dominate my experience. Let me go back to the beginning . . .

During our trip, we had the opportunity to purchase individual healing sessions with one of the three shamans (paqos) that accompanied our tour group. I jumped at the opportunity on the first day and, after Don Wilbert worked on me, he shared his observations. He saw how I had difficulty trusting, and he identified how I kept my heart closed and feared sharing my heart—my authentic self—fully with people. Yet at the same time he saw how porous my energy field was and told me, "It is too easy for people to get inside you." He counseled me to invoke my protections every day and encouraged me to give love, stay open, and not close my heart.

Intuitively, I asked him if I should call in Puma to help me with these heart teachings. "Yes!" he agreed, sharing a few more instructions and then telling me to "focus on the tail and the eyes."

In this region of Peru, the cosmology of the people includes a strong emphasis on the three worlds: Hanan Pacha, the upper world; Kay Pacha, the middle world; and Ukhu Pacha, the lower or inner world. Animal totems accompany each world: Condor in the Hanan Pacha, Puma in the Kay Pacha, and Serpent in the Ukhu Pacha. My intuition to call upon Puma came from knowing this association.

That afternoon, our paqos brought their wares to sell and I was immediately drawn to a puma staff, but my brain was hesitant because the stone puma head was black (pumas are golden). Yet I trusted my heart and purchased the staff. The puma had begun working me!

The next day our group participated in Shamanic Breathwork and in my journey a black panther came to me! She used to protect my apacheta *(outdoor altar made of stones) and told me that there is much more she could do for me if I would allow her. I eagerly consented and she proceeded to show me her medicine, giving me specific instructions on how to use her. She told me very clearly, "I will teach you how to live more from your heart, but first you must feel safe. I am here to protect you. I will always be with you and never leave you. I will walk on your right side and when you sleep at night I will lie next to you and curl my tail in a spiral around your heart."*

Tail! Don Wilbert had said to pay attention to the tail. How could he have known?! This was amazing. This beautiful black panther who showed herself to me was my "puma." And now I know why the puma staff I purchased had a black head. But the synchronicities and magic don't end there!

After Sacsayhuamán we had the opportunity to shop in Cuzco for a few hours. Vera made sure to take us all to the Shaman Shop and it was there I was stopped dead in my tracks at the likeness of my black panther on a drum that was hanging on the wall. Eyes . . . eyes! Don Wilbert had talked about the eyes!

Her golden eyes pierced my heart and I asked the store owner (who had also created the drum) if he would get it down for me. I stroked it, held it, and thumped on it with the drum beater. I hugged it close to my chest and wandered around the store with it, still altered from the day's events. It was expensive, and my head was hesitant to pay that much money for something this early in the trip. A friend suggested, "Just put it down and walk away and see how you feel." My eyes immediately grew huge, a lump formed in my throat, and I squawked, "I can't!"

There was my answer.

This magnificent creature is now part of my morning ritual as I beat my black panther drum and call in my daily protections as Don Wilbert advised. I'm still not completely clear why I had such an intense experience at Sacsayhuamán, but can only conclude it was part of my initiation into Puma medicine, heart medicine. As the saying goes, "The longest journey you will ever take is from your head to your heart." By the grace of Peru and my black panther, I am one step closer.

SHAMANIC JOURNEY

KAY PACHA—FINDING THE WISDOM
OF YOUR GREAT WITHIN
Guided by Vera Lopez

Take a deep breath. Exhale fully. Close your eyes, and breathe deeply into your lungs. Fill your lungs with oxygen and exhale fully, pushing out any resistance, and blockages, and hindrances to this present moment. Feel your grounding cord extend from the base of your spine and drop all the way down to the Earth, connecting you to the core of Pachamama. Feel Pachamama receive your grounding cord, and feel her hold and anchor you to this time, to this space, and to this dimension. With each inhale you pull up the grounding energy provided by Pachamama, and with each exhale you release and let go of any and all distractions.

Continue to breathe and feel yourself become more grounded, more centered in this present moment and within your physical body. Notice how your body feels sitting or lying down. Scanning your body, use your breath to support and nurture any areas of tension it may hold. Allow your body to fully relax and surrender into this journey—this journey into the heart.

Once your body is relaxed, project your spirit into the sacred lands of Peru. These lands are filled with jungles, mountains, and rivers, and each of these terrains is home to a wide range of wildlife. Envision your spirit being in these sacred lands, walking along the banks of the great Urubamba River. As you walk upon the banks of this river you observe the rapid flow of water moving around and through the ancient boulders that were once held within the mountaintops above. The river flows like a large silver anaconda winding its way throughout the jungles of Peru. Walking along the banks, you look above and see a condor fly out from the trees. It glides effortlessly throughout the sky and then disappears into the mists, soaring through the portals between this world and the otherworld.

The path along the river bends and turns around, and as you turn, you see Puma sitting upon a rock in the center of the moving river. Puma sees you, and looks directly at you, almost as if it were waiting for you to arrive—almost as if you both have a date together that has been written in the stars. You move closer to the puma, and see that there is a path of stones leading out to the rock the puma is on. Carefully and slowly you make your way—rock by rock—to the same stone that holds Puma.

Upon reaching the center stone, you slowly sit down across from Puma, locking eyes. As you peer into the puma's eyes and the puma stares into yours, there is an intense flow of energy. This flow of energy opens your heart and you begin to dive deep into the center of your heart chakra. Breathing into your heart space, the puma guides you through the pathways of your heart. It shows you your values, your dreams, your passions, and guides you to your holy longing.

Puma moves through your heart with such grace and majesty, its body strong and muscular, its eyes and presence unwavering with love and compassion. As Puma moves through your heart, it begins to purify the energies within it. It removes heartache, dissolves pain; it opens your heart to be able to receive and hold more love and compassion for yourself and others in the world. As Puma moves through your heart, it begins to awaken its energies. It stirs up your passion, it revitalizes your creativity, and it awakens the innate gifts and frequencies found within your heart center.

Breathing deeply into your heart, use your breath to expand your heart's center. Use your breath to open up your heart and enliven the frequencies found and stirred up by the Great Puma. Use your breath to connect with the values in your heart—what do you hold most sacred in life? What is sacred to you? What sparks your passion, and what feeds your heart and soul? Breathe into these questions, and allow the guardian spirit of Puma to guide you.

Following the guidance of Puma, see and notice the condition of your heart now that it has been cleansed and purified. See if you can find a word, a symbol, or an image that captures the condition of your heart. What medicine does your heart hold for you in this current moment?

Take some time to connect to all of these energies and feel them come to life as you place your attention upon them. Be still within your heart and see what medicine and messages you find.

After you've had some time to drop into your heart, gather up any pieces of medicine that want to come back with you from this experience. Perhaps there was medicine in the Puma's purification process, or maybe medicine was found deep within your heart, only to come to the surface after breathing deeply into these energies. Whatever is present within your heart—your Great Within—bring it to your consciousness; bring it to your awareness.

Thank Puma for its purification and its guidance, knowing that this creature has become an astral ally for you and you can return to work with it any time you wish. Take a deep breath and exhale fully. Carrying the medicine that you've found, come back to your body, and come back to this time and to this space. Breathe into your body. Wiggle your fingers and toes. Remember your pieces of medicine, bringing them back into this time and into this dimension. And when you feel ready, open your eyes.

Take some time to journal about your experience. Record your journey in a sacred journal or diary, or create an art piece or an art mandala to ground your experience into this reality.

HUMMINGBIRD MEDICINE

The Legend of Siwar Q'enti

The Andean natives, like all indigenous nations and cultures around the world, honor and respect life in all of its forms. For these ancient and indigenous cultures, everything upon our planet embodies a spark of life. Plants, trees, animals, stones, rivers, oceans, and even us human beings are believed to hold a divine essence, an energy that unites us all together within the web of life.

For the Inca, all living kingdoms are important and equal. In their eyes, there is no hierarchy for life. The mineral kingdom is just as important as the animal kingdom, as is the plant kingdom. There is truly no division between life; rather, there is a deep relationship with all Creation.

We see this deep relationship with all of life manifest within the Andean cosmology—the people of the Andes use the snake, the condor, and the puma as personifications, or symbols, of their core beliefs and values. Snake represents the Ukhu Pacha and symbolizes life's ability to change and transform. Condor represents the Hanan Pacha and teaches us how to rise out of our own personal stories and see the bigger picture. Puma represents the Kay Pacha and symbolizes the strength and beauty that reside within one's own heart and spirit.

The ancient Andean people highly honored and revered these three animals. The Andean people built entire cities and sacred temples using these three animals as models. For example, the original layout of Cuzco was built to model the body shape of a puma. The Serpent of Light temple in the Sacred Valley models the shape of a snake. And Machu Picchu—the pinnacle of sacred sites within the Andes Mountains—was built to model the shape of a hummingbird.

While the hummingbird does not personify or represent one of the three worlds within the Andean cosmology, the hummingbird does hold deep significance within Andean culture. In one of my first journeys to Peru, an elder shared with me the legend of Siwar Q'enti (which is "hummingbird" in Quechua).

This elder first taught me about the sacred medicine of each animal of the sacred trilogy—Snake, Puma, and Condor—explaining that these animals bless the life of people every day with their presence, and the union of these three creatures creates the Andean path to enlightenment.

"The snake dreams to gain legs and become a puma. The puma dreams of growing wings so it can fly high like the condor. And the Inca, they dream of becoming the hummingbird," the elder shared with me.

Humans have been fascinated by hummingbirds for centuries. There is definitely something magical about this little winged creature, which makes it like no other creature living upon our planet. Hummingbirds can fly fast through the air—backward, forward, or just hovering in midair. Their wings beat up to eighty times per second, creating a humming sound similar to bees and other insects. In Peru there are more than 120 different species of hummingbird—fourteen of these species can be found only in Peru.

"Why would the Inca—one of Earth's greatest civilizations—dream of becoming a hummingbird?" I asked the elder.

The elder continued by sharing the Andean legend of the hummingbird.

Siwar Q'enti, the hummingbird, heard that Kuntur—the Great Condor—was the messenger between the people of Earth and Viracocha, the god of Creation. Only the Great Condor could fly high enough to speak to the source of all of life.

One day Siwar Q'enti asked Kuntur if he could hide himself within the wings of the condor and fly with him to the Hanan Pacha—the world of the gods. Siwar Q'enti told Kuntur that he was a hummingbird—tiny and light—and he would not disturb the Great Condor during his flight; he only wished to see the face of Viracocha.

Kuntur immediately replied by saying, "No! This is not possible. I am the only being allowed to enter the Hanan Pacha, and not even I am allowed to look at Viracocha. When I speak to him I turn my face away so that our gaze never meets. This is the respectful way to honor the god of Creation."

With the purest of hearts and intentions, Siwar Q'enti could not understand why he could not look into the eyes of the Creator. He was a focused little hummingbird, and he was determined to find his way to the upper world—the Hanan Pacha.

The next day, Kuntur prepared himself to fly to the upper world. He gathered the prayers of all the people and began to make his flight. While Kuntur was preparing himself, Siwar Q'enti quietly snuck himself under the wing of the Great Condor, hitching a free ride to the Hanan Pacha and to Viracocha. Kuntur soared high up into the air. He was so focused on his mission to reach the Hanan Pacha and deliver the prayers that he did not notice the little hummingbird hiding beneath his wings.

Kuntur arrived at the Hanan Pacha and he delivered the prayers to Viracocha, making sure that he did not face or look at the god of Creation. As Kuntur was getting ready to speak to Viracocha, both Kuntur and Viracocha were startled by the sound of a humming buzz.

Before Kuntur could speak, Siwar Q'enti flew out from underneath the condor's wing and quickly made his way to Viracocha—facing the god of Creation head on. Looking directly into the eyes of Viracocha, Siwar Q'enti instantly changed colors and became luminous as a brilliant gold.

By becoming this brilliant gold color, Siwar Q'enti was transformed. He not only changed into a golden hummingbird, he also became Korinti, the holy golden hummingbird.

"So the Inca wanted to become gold?" I asked the elder.

"No," he replied, "they wanted to become as pure as the hummingbird. Only a creature with a pure heart and an innocent soul could look into the eyes of the Creator and reflect his light."

This legend of Siwar Q'enti demonstrates the tenacity and power of hummingbird medicine. Through this legend we learn how to look for the gifts within every situation—the dark and the light. We must be able to, like the hummingbird, find the sweetness in life. For life's sweetness is the nectar that feeds our hearts and our souls.

This is the power of hummingbird medicine—it's learning how to find and celebrate joy regardless of our life circumstances and experience. In Peru, shamans call upon the energies of Korinti, the golden hummingbird, as they believe that the hummingbird, like the Great Condor, is a bridge between the worlds. Peruvian shamans believe that hummingbirds take the beauty, pureness, peace, and love from the upper world and share these energies with all of life on Earth. This is another potent piece of hummingbird medicine— learning how to journey into upper realms of consciousness to find the wisdom within the bigger picture, and bringing this information and wisdom back down into our everyday lives. The spirit of the hummingbird teaches us how to find joy and how to fly between the worlds.

➤➤◄◄

STAR WOLF SPEAKS

THE THREE WORLDS OF SHAMANIC CONSCIOUSNESS AND THE ANDEAN COSMOLOGY

In traditions all around the world we see the beliefs associated with different realms of existence—different worlds of life and consciousness.

In the Christian tradition, there is the framework of heaven, hell, and earth. In various shamanic traditions, there are the lower, upper, and middle worlds. Today in our modern-day consciousness we have the awareness of multidimensionality or otherworlds of existence outside of our physical time and space. We are even discovering the various worlds within our own body—our emotional body, our mental body, and even the microbiomes inside of our gut.

The main point is to understand that human beings have long been aware of and contemplated the different layers and levels of existence. Whether you choose to look at these different worlds as literal worlds of existence or metaphoric representations of the psyche, it is the experience of consciousness that makes them real. These various worlds, levels, and dimensions provide human beings with the ability to create morals, laws, and codes of ethics. Through the exploration of the lower worlds and the upper worlds, and the integration of the two in our present-day middle world, we are able to develop and discern an awareness about what actions and behaviors are "right" and which ones are "wrong."

Tapping into the Peruvian cosmology we can see a variation of the three worlds illustrated in the Ukhu Pacha, the Kay Pacha, and the Hanan Pacha. These three worlds are represented by Serpent, Puma, and Condor. Each of these animals, of course, represents and personifies the energies of these three different worlds of existence, or levels of consciousness.

Serpent, or Snake, representing the Ukhu Pacha, is the same serpentine energy represented throughout time and prevalent in the cosmology of many other cultures around the world. It is the same serpent found in the Garden of Eden, it is the same energy as our kundalini life-force energy, and it is the same Serpent who is also known as the Great Wisdom Serpent in indigenous cultures.

An older symbol of the serpent shares how it is an archetype for transformation and the process of becoming a new creature by shedding one's skin. Whether Serpent has been cast as a demon or a god, this serpentine force runs throughout each of our bodies. It speaks to and represents our lower base chakra energies of survival, sexuality, and power.

The serpent represents our innate human drives that keep us alive and physically present on our planet. Working with Serpent energy provides us with the energy to create life, generate transformation, and discover ourselves as human beings.

Condor symbolizes the energies of the upper world—the Hanan Pacha in Peru. Condor is the energy that can rise high above the Andes. It is the highest-flying bird, so it has the association and connection with the unseen worlds above. Condor is also a bird that eats death, thus some of Condor's energies involve learning how to take death and digest it into life.

In the Andes, it's believed that when we shed our physical bodies and journey into the other world, it is Condor who greets us and takes us to the land of the dead. Outside of these associations, Condor reminds us to always look to the Great Above and connect to the beings living in these unseen dimensions of the upper worlds and in the Great Star Nation. In so doing, we connect with these beings and bring down the wisdom of their larger vision, their higher intelligence, onto Earth, thereby informing the serpent.

Serpent and Condor are in constant dialogue with one another. They support and feed off one another, and according to the cosmology of the Andes people, the early Inca felt it was necessary to have a third world, a world that integrates and unifies the energies of the lower realms and the upper realms—a world that is fit for humankind.

The Kay Pacha, or this world, really has to do with being human. The Kay Pacha is represented by Puma. Even though the puma is a four-legged creature, it still relates to and symbolizes the journey of the human. If humans bend down and walk, they are doing so on all fours. Some researchers even say that humans moved around on all fours before we stood up and became human. So this warm-blooded, four-legged creature that walks upon the Earth—this mammal—is connected to the human being, and we find this connection throughout many cultures around the world. In some cultures, this animal is the lion and in others it is the wolf.

The shared commonality is that the creature who represents humanity and this physical existence of consciousness is commonly represented as a predator species. We can learn a lot by examining this symbolic representation, for the predator of any species does not kill for sport; it only kills for safety and survival. This apex predator lives by some code of ethics—some awareness—that brings the consciousness of the lower world (our survival needs and instincts) and merges them with the wisdom and knowledge found in the upper worlds. This predator lives its life by a sort of standard of awareness and it knows that what happens to the world around it—the whole—directly affects every individual.

So to me, Puma is really an integration or unification of the upper and lower worlds. Puma embodies the wisdom and needs of the serpent in the Ukhu Pacha and it listens to and acknowledges the wisdom of the upper world—the Hanan Pacha and Condor. This warm-blooded, four-legged creature of the heart brings the energies of both of these worlds and walks with them in its daily life. To walk with the energies of Puma is to really learn how to walk with the energies and consciousness of both worlds and integrate them within the heart.

In the Wolf Clan Teachings of Grandmother Twylah, the wolf embodies these same energies. Wolf looks to the stars and calls these energies from the Great Above, and at the same time it can be a fierce warrior when it needs to protect, when it needs to defend, and when it needs to hunt. Wolf, like Puma, can pull up and catalyze all of the base chakra (survival) energies.

Looking at the cosmology of Peru, we can examine how these different worlds or levels of consciousness can influence our everyday life. We know how to walk with our human needs and desires, and we are able to embody and integrate the love and wisdom of Puma as well as of Snake and Condor. In merging these three worlds—the As Above, the So Below, and the Great Within—and connecting them in the heart, we can walk our path and journey in balance with these energies and with the worlds around us.

⏵⏵◀◀

SHAMANIC JOURNEY
THROUGH THE THREE WORLDS
Guided by Star Wolf

Take a deep breath. Exhale fully and begin a journey that's been calling you for a long time—a journey that's leading you to an ancient time and an ancient wisdom. Breathing in and breathing out fully, feel your heart beating and your bare feet walking on a path through the jungle, through the lower lands. You hear thunder and a gentle rain begins.

Condor flies overhead; broad wings flying upward, over the distant mountains. As it flies, it flies into the clouds and the rain—disappearing out of sight—disappearing perhaps into other dimensions. It is gathering the wisdom of the Great Mystery, the Great Spirit, from the Unseen Ones that live in the heaven worlds and sending back inspiration, messages, for how to live our lives; how to live in harmony, in peace. It is relaying knowledge about how to know when to grow the crops, to build homes, and to move to higher ground when the rains are coming. All these things Condor tells us from the Great Above if we know how to listen. And when it's time to lay our bodies down, our spirits are called home; carried by the great ones—the Great Condors—back to the heavenly realms to join our brothers and sisters, and become the ancestors; sending our wisdom back to Earth to those who remain below.

Winding around the path moving through the jungle, past the Urubamba River, the Great Serpent appears, snaking its way through the Andes. We remember the energies of the Great Serpent itself—the one from the Great Below, rumpling beneath the Earth and rising up to its surface. Powerful and strong, undulating through the tall grass among the rocks, winding itself to the river to take a drink to fill itself, to quench its thirst. We remember that this great being reminds us of our connection to our bodies and to this Earth; that we are hungry, that we are thirsty, that we need to co-create, to shed our old ways, our old skins. The Great Serpent reminds us how to renew ourselves each day on our earthly walk upon this Earth; how to tend to the most basic drives and needs; how to let that powerful energy rise up within us, and to find our creativity; creating perhaps pottery in the ancient ways from the clay found beside the river and among the stones, painting arrows, painting caves, painting our bodies.

The Great Serpent reminds us when it's time to keep moving, to keep transforming, to not stay in any place too long (any place in our consciousness, that is). We are reminded that the great wheel turns on a spiral dance, and just as the serpent coils up on the warm rocks by the river to sun itself, perhaps dreaming a new dream, we too follow the coiling serpentine energy. We do this to remember where we've been, where we're going, and to recognize the path on our spiral journey.

We then move into the energy that unites the Great Condor and the Great Serpent, the energy of the powerful, graceful Puma. Some call the jaguar the great cat, the four-legged one, the one that is perhaps more closely related to the human: warm-blooded, with the need to care for its young; to care for its land, for its home. The human can contemplate and imagine the two worlds—Above and Below—that unite and live within itself.

Puma has wise eyes; heightened senses of smell, taste, and hearing; a strong heart beating in its chest; a muscular body, in this case still covered with fur, replaced by clothing in human beings perhaps. This great one knows how to keep the balance between the worlds . . . How to acknowledge its own boundaries and territories, and balance that with acknowledging others . . . How to find shelter from the storm. The powerful Puma listens to its brother and sister, Condor and Serpent, but walks its own path and discovers new truths about what it means to be one who walks upon this Earth, seeking the balance of the Above and the Below and in the Within.

And so we learn from these creatures. We learn from these dimensions and we know that as human beings we are all three. And when any of these worlds are out of balance, we are out of balance, and we must seek to restore the three worlds within us, honoring the Above, the Below, and the Within.

Take a moment to feel that restoration within yourself, just breathing in and breathing out. And if there's a message, let it come now. Perhaps only one speaks to you, or two or all three, but listen and receive the message, the message intended for you to restore the balance of your own oath. Take a deep breath and exhale fully, and bring that message into full consciousness and awareness as you return to the present moment.

KARPAYS

Initiations of Shamanic Peru

The experience in Peru—this experience with nature and man's relationship to it—is based on generations of Andean men and women.

VERA LOPEZ

INITIATION IS DEFINED as the process of admitting a person into a group or belief system through a ritual or ceremony. This process welcomes the initiate into a formal lineage—an etheric connection that unites initiates together with other initiates as well as with all the ancestors of the tradition. More often than not, it greatly influences and impacts the life of the person being initiated.

In Peru, the paqos—the medicine men of the Andes—undergo and offer a series of initiatory rites called *karpays*. A karpay is a transmission wherein a paqo (an Incan priest) intercedes on one's behalf by invoking the elemental beings to assist in the shift—from the human beings we are to the luminous beings we are all becoming. This is done by planting an intentional, luminous seed that literally infuses itself into our DNA. This seed, once given to us by them and fed by us, will grow in our energetic field; it is there to assist us in our transformative process. The three karpays (or initiations) of the Q'eros people are:

- Llankay
- Munay
- Yachay

Similar to the beliefs of Eastern yogis and mystics who posit that we have seven points of power residing in our energetic body (the chakras), the paqos of the Andes believe that the body is comprised of three energetic levels. Within each of these levels reside seeds of energy pertaining to service, love, and wisdom. These three places of power are our groin region, our heart center, and the crown of our head. During the karpay initiations, the paqos clear out these energy centers in the body and activate the seeds of potential that live therein.

In addition to activating the three levels of our energy field, the karpay initiations also gift us with a transmission of shamanic wisdom, knowledge, and power. When the paqos gift someone with a karpay initiation, they are also gifting that person with the generations of knowledge and wisdom that have energetically been passed down through the ages. When you receive a karpay, you receive the medicine of the Q'eros nation. In addition, you are receiving a lineage that is generations old. With each process and transmission, you are being activated to a greater level and understanding of service, love, and wisdom. In this you become an ambassador of the Earth—you become a wisdom keeper and a medicine carrier of the Q'eros nation.

LLANKAY KARPAY

Llankay can be roughly translated as "work" or "service" toward all living creations and the universe (Cosmos, "Source," Creator, etc.). Llankay is a state of consciousness in which each individual's soul purpose, or path in life, is in service to their fellow human beings as well as the cosmos. Everything that we "do" is in ultimate service to the Divine.

If we look at the first three chakras, we can see that these first three points of power—the root chakra, the sacral chakra, and the solar plexus chakra—all support us in grounding to this physical reality. They center us and inspire us to take actions in the world that sustain us and our life force. These lower energies are held within the groin region of the physical body and correspond to the Llankay Karpay. When this energy center is activated or awakened, it indicates that we are in service, and by being in service, we are in alignment with llankay.

When we receive our Llankay Karpay we enter the initiation of discovering our sacred purpose—the niche or role that our soul is destined to fulfill and provide to the world. Some people think that being in service is focused on the action of giving and receiving, but in Peru, this is not the case. For the paqos and the Quechua people living in the Andes, service is the energy that moves one to action and begins one's maturation journey. In receiving the llankay initiation you understand that you are no longer going to be provided for—you must provide for yourself, take care of yourself, and begin the journey of your sacred path; you must start walking the path of your sacred purpose and generate your service within the world.

Llankay allows us to express our creativity through our work and can also be thought to symbolize the power of the physical body, or our animal selves. Llankay explains that we are all one part of a bigger picture and that each part—each of us—is inherently dependent on the other. We all have a sacred purpose within the bigger picture. We all have a role to play and a niche to fulfill, and our sacred niche supports the whole. With llankay, we know that we are not alone. The lesson of llankay is "We are all connected."

INITIATION
LLANKAY KARPAY
Guided by Vera Lopez

Take a deep breath and exhale fully. Take another deep breath, exhale fully, and close your eyes. Prepare your body, mind, and spirit to undergo a timeless initiation from an ancient lineage . . .

With your eyes closed, imagine an Incan priest—a paqo—coming to you now. As this priest comes closer to you, you can see and feel his generosity, his humility, and his immense knowledge rooted within him and connected to generations before his own. This Incan priest has traveled throughout time and space to be with you today—to guide you through and share with you an ancient initiation of the soul—the Llankay Karpay.

Take a deep breath and open your heart to this beautiful being before you. As you continue to breathe, open your heart and feel yourself become fully present in this moment. The paqo begins to invoke the elemental beings of earth, air, fire, water, and spirit. He calls upon the Apus—the spirits of the mountains and great lakes—and welcomes their presence in this ceremony.

He finishes calling in the Apurunas, the spirits of nature, and he calls in the ancestors as he approaches you with his mesa—an altar of sacred objects bundled together within a sacred cloth. He touches your heart with his mesa—transmitting power through the vibrational frequencies of the holy stones and sacred medicine in his sacred altar. He looks deeply into your eyes and you look deeply into his. Feeling this connection between the two of you, the paqo begins to pray in his ancient language, Quechua—the language of the people of the high Andes. This language sounds almost otherworldly to you, and as you listen to his prayers you begin to feel yourself open to the universe, and deeply connected to Source.

As you continue to breathe and tune into these timeless and ancient vibrations, your connection to Source deepens, and you begin to feel the path of life opening up before you. As this path opens, you obtain a strong sense of clarity around your soul's purpose and you remember this innate knowing: We are all connected to a deep sense of planetary service.

Take a moment and feel into your soul's purpose now. What does it feel like? How is this purpose manifesting, or wanting to manifest, in your life? What are the gifts that you have within you that you can offer and share with the world?

The paqo continues to chant his prayers—invoking the energies of the Llankay Karpay—and you feel your vibrational energy body shift. You notice that your body and soul begin emanating a brilliant white light, and this white light extends outward as a thread. You follow this thread of light and see that it is connected to a giant web of light suspended within the cosmos. Intuitively you know that this web of light is the web of life—the energetic tapestry of all of Creation. And as you take in this magnificent site, you begin to realize that you and your soul's purpose are part of a much larger story—you are a vital piece within the bigger picture that is unfolding.

Breathe into this connection—the connection to your soul's purpose and understand how your soul's purpose is woven into the cosmic web of life. As you breathe and feel into these connections, you notice beings of light emerging from around you.

These beings of light match the same white light beaming from the cosmic web before you, and you know that these beings of light are your ancestors—the ancestors of your past and of your present.

They have come to support and congratulate you on receiving this ancient initiation of planetary service, and as they circle around you they each begin to send a beam of white light from their heart center. These beams of light find their way into your own heart space—weaving together the collective presence and support you have available to you throughout time and space. This energy fills your heart, and you know that you are supported, you are guided, and you are loved.

The paqo finishes his prayers. You and he express your gratitude and appreciation to all the spirits of nature and ancestors for being present for your first journey within the Andean priesthood—the Llankay Karpay. You and he begin to walk away from the cosmic web of life and all the ancestors from the past and future. As you journey back into your present time and space, you know that you are always connected to these universal energies—you feel these energies and their light within your heart center.

You turn to face the beautiful paqo—your guide and initiator. You thank him for sharing this initiation with you and for opening the door to the ancestral and spiritual realms. You bow your head in gratitude and acknowledge that the energies you received and accessed today are now seeds within your heart, which you pledge to cultivate and grow through your actions of service and compassion in your everyday life. You know that from this day forward you are an awakened planetary change-agent and you are in service to your greatest self, your community, and your planet. Through your soul-inspired contributions of love and service, you will ground and anchor the light frequencies within this dimension, thereby supporting the elevation and expansion of the collective consciousness.

Take a deep breath and begin to feel your body. Wiggle your fingers and toes, and feel yourself return back into this time and space—bringing with you all the gifts and experiences you received from this journey. Feel yourself return, and when you feel ready, open your eyes and journal your experience.

MUNAY KARPAY

If there is an English word to describe munay, the closest word would be *love,* and more specifically, *unconditional love.* Munay is the greatest vibration of love; it holds a consciousness of acceptance and appreciation for all Creation and all that is. As you grow in your understanding of your llankay and begin to journey up toward your initiation of munay, you are beginning to understand that "what" you are doing in service to yourself, your community, and to the world—your sacred purpose—must be met and carried through your heart. Your llankay must be fused with your munay, your sense of love and appreciation for all that is. The Andes people believe you cannot do true service if your service is not coming from your heart.

Accordingly, the seeds of munay reside within our heart chakra—the fourth energy center of the chakras situated around the region of our physical heart. Like the heart chakra, munay bridges our lower self with our higher self; it is the center that holds us together. In the heart it integrates the wisdom of our higher self and merges it together with the desires of our physical human form.

To access the seeds of our munay—the highest vibration of love—we must clear the pathways of our heart. In our modern world, we have expressions such as a *broken heart* or a *heavy heart.* These expressions indicate that our heart holds an immense amount of heavy, dense energy and emotions that weigh us down. Some of these energies and emotions are anger, sadness, resentment, depression, and anxiety.

While experiencing these emotions is a function of our humanity, the Andes people do not believe that our hearts should always carry them. They believe that our hearts are a vessel designed to only hold love. Because the heart is a leading voice in the shamanic traditions of the Andes, the Andes people do their best to clear their heart centers each and every day. This means that munay, while being an initiation and an activation that one can receive, is also a lifestyle that is intended to be embodied and practiced each and every day.

While the seeds of munay may be activated through an initiation, it is up to us to tend these seeds—to nurture them, feed them, and support them as they grow and germinate. By doing so, we can infuse their energies of great love and wisdom into our life and our actions.

The lesson of munay is "We are one."

INITIATION
MUNAY KARPAY
Guided by Vera Lopez

We are ready for our next transmission of power.

We breathe deeply and connect to the shamanic energies of the Munay Karpay. Munay is a consciousness that comes from within us—it is an acceptance and an appreciation of the entire universe. Munay is how we receive and give, how we breathe in and breathe out. Munay is unconditional love.

Take a moment to envision and connect to the energy of munay—this energy of unconditional love. As you open your heart to this energy and consciousness, the paqo approaches you. His luminous body is shining with the light of a million stars. As he draws closer, he too opens his heart and shares his loving kindness with you as you wait to receive the Munay Karpay.

The paqo leans down and shares with you that you are ready to move upward along your journey and that it is time for you to receive a deep understanding of love. You place your hands on your heart, and he begins to pray in Quechua—invoking the blessings of munay upon you.

As the ancient vibrations of his prayers fill your ears and ring throughout your body, you notice that your heart field begins to grow and expand. Your heart begins to open up to the universe and you begin to connect with the loving energies of Father Sky. You breathe deeply and your heart expands further to hold the nurturing energies of Mother Earth. You feel this integration of *as above, so below* occur within your heart center and you breathe this sacred union into each cell of your body.

You open and stretch out your arms and allow the loving energies of the universe to flow throughout your body, mind, and spirit. This is your true essence, this is your core—love. Breathe into this knowing and remember the vibration of your soul and spirit.

This is the munay initiation—it is a coming back home to our own heart and remembering the love that is our truest essence. This karpay and initiation is an invitation to step forward and bring greater love into our everyday lives. It is a blessing of our hands so that each of our actions is based on our heart's wisdom. It is a blessing of the mouth so that our words speak more love into our life and into the lives of others. Munay is a connection to our core so that through our hands, our hearts, and our minds we embody the fullest expression of who we truly are.

Take a moment to breathe into this remembering, and allow the vibrations of love to fill and move through you.

You return your hands to your heart and see the paqo standing before you, smiling with joy. You thank the paqo and you bow your heads to each other. The paqo walks away and begins to fade into the distant landscape.

You breathe deeply and feel into the blessings of this initiation—the vibrations and frequencies of love still pulsing throughout your body and illuminating your heart. You know with every fiber of your being that this transmission has shifted something within you; it has opened you to a deeper connection to love. This connection will forever be with you and it will be felt by others as you journey forth throughout the world.

Take a deep breath, and ground this loving energy into your physical body. Feel yourself return to your time, space, and dimension. Wiggle your fingers and toes, and when you feel ready, open your eyes. Journal about your journey and record your experiences.

YACHAY KARPAY

The third karpay initiation is *yachay*. *Yachay* translates to mean "wisdom"—the wisdom is of an inner knowing and a connection to the higher consciousness of our "authentic" or true selves. It understands that we are not our egos; we are so much more. Yachay is the initiation that activates and awakens the seeds of our highest self.

When our llankay—the seeds of service and sacred purpose—and our munay—the seeds of love and appreciation for all that is—are in balance and in right relationship with one another, we are able to experience the enlightening energies of yachay.

The seeds of yachay are stored in our third eye and crown chakras. When these seeds are activated and awakened we are able to connect to the greater vision of our lives—we can see that everything truly is connected and harmoniously orchestrated to support our growth and development on planet Earth. As these seeds of yachay grow and take root, we begin to remember the true essence of who we are. We are able to receive cosmic downloads from the Great Above, and we are able to form strong connections with our spiritual allies in other realms and dimensions.

Yachay allows us to transcend our ego identities and experience the freedom that comes when we embody our truest essence, our higher self. When we are living in alignment with yachay we are able to remain in a state of inner peace and joy regardless of whatever strife or turmoil is occurring in our lives. Yachay grants us the ability to see life through the lens of the Great Above and because of this perspective we are able to remain connected to a state of stillness and presence.

The lesson and medicine of yachay teach us that "All is well."

Each of these initiations, or karpays, are done in alignment with ayni—the law of reciprocity. These initiations are the processes and pathways of life for the Q'eros people. Living in accordance and in alignment with each of these karpays connects us to the realization that we are not separate from life and one another. When we are able to activate the seeds of service, love, and wisdom within ourselves and carry this medicine and awareness with us each and every day, we are able to anchor more love and consciousness upon our planet. By awakening and embodying these energies within ourselves, we become ambassadors of the Earth and hold the portals of transformation open for our planet and all living beings.

INITIATION
YACHAY KARPAY
Guided by Vera Lopez

Take a deep breath, and exhale fully. Take another deep breath, exhale fully, and close your eyes. As you continue to breathe deeply, I invite you to relax your body—sending deep breaths of oxygen to each muscle in your body, allowing the muscles to release any tension and relax. Breathe deeply into your mind, and use your exhale to still any racing thoughts, allowing yourself to become fully present in the present moment. Breathe into your heart, relaxing and opening your heart field.

You are now ready to journey into the next initiation of the shamanic mysteries of Peru—the Yachay Karpay.

Your friend and cosmic brother—the paqo—comes back to you. You smile at his familiar face, and as he draws closer to you, you can sense the depth of his ancient lineage. He stands before you, smiles, and places his hands over the top of your head and begins to pray in Quechua.

His language is like a mantra—activating your soul and expanding your consciousness. And while he is speaking in a different language, you can intuitively understand him—for the language of the ancient Andes is not based on definitions and meanings of words and language. It is a language based on the emotions and the felt-sense of the heart.

You breathe into your heart space and you feel into the vibrations of the paqo's timeless prayers, and you know that you are ready to receive the third initiation. For when the llankay and munay are in balanced relationship in our being we are ready to receive entry into the law of yachay.

The paqo invokes the presence of the ancestors and the nature spirits—calling upon the Apus of the mountains, rivers, oceans, trees, and other elemental beings. You breathe in and welcome the presence of these ancient and timeless beings, and the paqo begins to invoke the energies of the Yachay Karpay above your crown chakra.

You go deep within your being and connect to your core essence—your truth and your inner spirit. The energies of yachay comprise our inner knowing; it is our inner guidance system that is always connected to higher consciousness. This knowing does not come from a place of the ego; rather it is rooted within the wisdom of the soul.

Breathe into this connection to your own inner guidance—to your soul's wisdom—and feel the depth of this wisdom encompassing and connected to the wisdom and knowledge of the cosmos—the Akashic Records, the star nations, and the wisdoms of the Earth and elements. We have all of these energies available to us when we are truly connected to our greater and unified selves. All we have to do is trust and know that the wisdom we seek lies within.

The paqo begins to bless you—using his rattle and drum to activate your energy body. And as he continues his Quechua chants you feel the wind begin to intensify, swirling cosmic dust around you and activating all of your chakra centers with this powerful connection to cosmic consciousness.

Within your third eye you see the lineage of your soul and you remember who you truly are—a Child of the Sun; a cosmic being of light, love, and wisdom, supporting the evolution and expansion of consciousness on planet Earth.

Take a moment to connect with your ancestry; connect with the wisdom innately within you, and breathe into your own knowing, your own inner guidance.

The paqo continues to chant, and within this space of connection and communion with the cosmic consciousness you make a vow to the paqo, the universe, and yourself. You vow that as you walk upon the Earth, you will be in service and in full alignment with your divine purpose. You vow to support the evolution of consciousness upon our planet, and you vow to honor your own lineage of ancestors, sages, and ancient medicine peoples who have come before you and are trusting you with these ancient mysteries. You make the vow in your heart to mirror and honor the beauty of all that you have received during your lifetime, and know that you are ready to become the next carrier of these wise and ancient teachings.

The paqo completes his prayers and invocations, and you have received the essence of the yachay initiation. Your third eye illuminates your thoughts with inspiration and visions to move you forward, held within the power of now. You breathe deeply and know with every fiber of your being that all is well and that everything is unfolding with divine alignment. You are connected, you are powerful, and you are love.

You open your mind's eye and see the paqo smiling before you. You bow your head and smile in gratitude for this beautiful being and all that he has shared with you. The paqo turns and walks away, disappearing into the distant landscape.

You take a deep breath and exhale fully. You feel yourself still connected to the freshness of your experience, and you bring it all back into your physical body. Wiggle your fingers and toes, and open your eyes when you are ready. Journal about your journey and record your experiences as you integrate your Yachay Karpay.

INITIATION BY LIGHT AND FIRE

Another form of initiation found in the Andes, and truly in indigenous cultures across the world, is the initiation of being struck by lightning. Across the world there is a common belief that a person can become a shaman by surviving the following three experiences: a severe illness, a near-death experience, and a lightning strike. These three experiences are known as life initiations, all of which are unplanned by the human psyche and orchestrated by a much larger force.

These experiences radically change a person's life—they truly undergo a death and rebirth experience. In the early cultures of our world, the people who survived these highly charged experiences were believed to possess the ability to journey between life and death, communicate with the spirits, and embody special supernatural powers. The following piece is a real-life story of Star Wolf and her initiation by light and fire.

>>◀◀

STRUCK BY THE LIGHT OF THE GODS

In my life, I've had the opportunity to experience and undergo several shamanic initiations along my path, including being struck by lightning. In the Andes and in other shamanic cultures around the world, being struck by lightning is considered to be a sacred initiation by fire and light. Being struck by lightning is believed to indicate that the gods have chosen you to be a shaman.

On June 17, 2018, I was facilitating the final teaching of my month-long Shamanic Breathwork training program. This teaching focuses on the imaginal cells and how we as human beings can activate these imaginal cells living within us, thereby embodying our future selves in present reality. Imaginal cells are the cells that reside in caterpillars. These specific cells signal to the caterpillar when it's time to spin a cocoon and shape-shift into a butterfly. In human beings, there is a part of each one of us that has this ability to envision and embody our future selves. This aspect of ourselves is called imagination. Imagination is a powerful part of the human mind and spirit. Albert Einstein said that "Imagination is more important than knowledge. For knowledge is limited, whereas imagination embraces the entire world, stimulating progress, giving birth to evolution." In shamanic practices and traditions, imagination is one of our key tools for journeying and transformation.

So on this final day of teaching in my training program, I was teaching about the power of our imagination in the field and study of shamanism. My students, staff, and I were in our Air Temple—a spacious and open pavilion—on top of our Dove Mountain training site located in the mountains of western North Carolina. A storm had rolled in over the mountains during this teaching and we all were in the heart of the pouring rain, booming thunder, and flashes of lightning. I was holding a microphone and finishing the last pieces of my teaching when a flash of lightning entered our Air Temple and struck me.

Looking back to this exact moment, the only thing I can remember is the searing pain that coursed through my body. The pain felt similar to an electrical shock, only a million times more intense. It propelled me out of my body and the next thing I knew was that I was standing in the presence of a golden light. In this bright and cloud-like golden light I could sense, and actually see, the presence of other beings surrounding me.

These other beings were shimmering beings of light, and they shared the same shimmering-like appearance of mirages in the desert or a heat wave on a hot summer day. I couldn't tell if any of these beings were male or female, or if they had any other attributes other than being shimmering beings of light.

In this in-between world of golden light, the only thing that separated me from these shimmering light beings was a thin veil. These light beings and I were suspended in the air, hovering within the golden cloudy light of this otherworld. What ensued can only be described as a gestalt moment of recognition and understanding—meaning that my consciousness received and processed all of these different parts and pieces as one complete and whole understanding.

What happened next was a conversation held between these shimmering beings of light and me. The shimmering beings asked me one question, "Would you rather drop your physical body or remain in physical form but drop your old ego identity?"

Because this was a gestalt-like experience, I understood what they were asking me, all in one nonlinear moment. In this moment I understood that they were asking me if I wanted to stay here in this otherworld and die to being a human being or return to Earth to have more human experiences, knowing that my life would never be the same. Meaning, I would be required to drop my ego identity as "Linda Star Wolf" and step fully into the next octave of my being as a soul incarnated on planet Earth. In this moment, I remember there was no room for negotiation with these beings around this decision. I couldn't bargain or arrange a different contract. It was either die as a human being or return to Earth and be willing to drop my old ego identity.

Reflecting back on this near-death experience, I do not remember how long I was in this otherworld with these shimmering beings, nor do I remember what my decision was: to die or drop my old ego identity.

After the shimmering beings asked me their question, the next thing I remember was landing back in my body and feeling all kinds of pain coursing through my physical form. Coming back into my body, I remember thinking and hoping that no one around me would touch me because I was scared they would either get electrocuted through me or they would interfere with everything occurring on the other side with my spirit. I also felt that if they touched me, I would surely lose connection with this reality and my physical form. Eventually, I was able to get off the ground and back to my home safely.

As my psyche and I continued to come back from this experience, and process everything that had occurred in this short period of time, I found myself coming back to the question these beings had asked me: "Would you rather drop your physical body or remain in physical form but drop your old ego identity?"

To this day, I still have no memory of saying, "Yes, I'll go back and drop my old ego identity," but I trust that these beings must have read my mind or they knew the decision my soul needed, and sent me back to Earth in my physical body.

In the weeks and months that followed my lightning strike, it was apparent that my old ego identity was definitely dropped. My life began to rapidly change and different processes that I had been working through began to surface fully into the light. One example of this is seen in my decision to come fully forward about my relationship with a younger man. I had hesitations about doing so because of our age difference, and I was concerned about how other people were going to perceive our relationship. Coming back into my physical body, and releasing my old ego identity, I knew that it was time to admit that I was in love once again. My new ego identity and the next octave of my life were calling me forward, urging me to spread my wings and fly higher than I had ever imagined I could.

I know now that in most indigenous cultures around the world, being struck by lightning denotes that one has become a "shaman." When I journeyed to Peru, and I shared my experience with our shamanic guide, he told me that according to the Q'eros tradition, I had been chosen to be a shaman. He shared with me that in the Q'eros nation, certain shamans go into the high mountains and seek out the initiation of lightning. The Q'eros people believe that if the lightning strikes you it is considered to be a blessing that many people do not survive. If they do, they live with crippling or degenerative illness for the rest of their lives.

I truly believe that on June 17, 2018, I underwent a powerful shamanic initiation by light and fire. On this day the tower of my ego fell, and just like the Andean shamans tell us about the initiation by lightning, one day my life was this way, and after being struck by lightning, my life became a whole new world.

Today, I am living as one who has been initiated and struck by lightning. This initiation reminds me of the lyrics of one of my favorite Disney songs, "When You Wish Upon a Star." This "bolt out of the blue"—the lightning strike—changed my world forever. It gave me the courage to face an outer ego death. In this, it allowed me to fully step through the portals of initiation so that I may embody the next octave of my shamanic consciousness and live out the next physical journey that my soul contracted for this lifetime.

Plate 1. Receiving the karpays, shamanic initiations

Plate 2. Despacho altar honoring the reciprocity that connects all life

Plate 3. Vera Lopez standing in the mists of Machu Picchu

Plate 4. Linda Star Wolf and her late husband, Brad Collins, receiving the Q'eros initiations in Moray

Plate 5. Vera connecting with the spirit of Condor

Plate 6. Vera entering the doorway of Machu Picchu

Plate 7. The Inca at Inti Raymi, the Incan Sun Festival, giving thanks for the year's blessings and asking for blessings for the new year

Plate 8. The Coya, Incan Queen, honoring the celebration of Inti Raymi

Plate 9. Vera and her husband, Jim, at the Lemurian Temple of Love in Ollantaytambo

Plate 10. In the heart of ayni, the sacred law of reciprocity

Plate 11. Baptism at Machu Picchu

Plate 12. Shopping at the Pisac markets

Plate 13. Celebrating the site of Machu Picchu

Plate 14. From left to right: Vera, Star Wolf, Nikólaus Wolf, and Jasin Deegan at Machu Picchu

Plate 15. Honoring the Andean god Viracocha, creator of the universe

Plate 16. Machu Picchu, the Avalon of the Inca

Plate 17. Sunrise at Machu Picchu

Plate 18. The Temple of the Condor at Machu Picchu

Plate 19. Entering the cave of the Ukhu Pacha, the world of the Great Below

Plate 20. The Serpent of Light Temple in the Sacred Valley of the Inca

Plate 21. Q'eros shamans with Vera and Star Wolf

Plate 22. Fire ceremony in the heart of the labyrinth, Sacred Valley of the Inca

Plate 23. Our group deep within the heart of Moray

Plate 24. Meditating in the ruins of Machu Picchu

Plate 25. *As above, so below* in Machu Picchu

Plate 26. Imasumac, Vera's spiritual daughter

Plate 27. Vera in the streets of Ollantaytambo

Plate 28. Chuma, High Priestess of Machu Picchu

Plate 29. Offering prayers of gratitude and blessings of reciprocity in the Despacho ceremony

Plate 30. The Ayni Project

Plate 31. Shamans calling upon the Apus spirits

Plate 32. Adventuring with the locals of Cuzco

PART 2

THE SACRED LAND AND TEMPLES OF PERU

BUILDING WITH INTENTION

Landing Place of the Gods

THE ANCIENT INCA WERE PEOPLE OF INTENTION. Each action they took and put forth in the world had sacred meaning and was aligned with the values of their ancient culture. The ancient Inca were not a people who moved impulsively, nor did they move out of convenience. Rather, they moved forward with precision and purpose.

This way of living can be seen in each temple, sacred site, and city found in the ancient world of the Andes. Looking at the placement of each site, modern-day archaeologists are discovering that each one was constructed for a specific purpose and/or in alignment with certain astrological timing, a season, and/or energies of the Earth. These temples were not built overnight like many of our strip malls and skyscrapers are today. Instead, they were constructed in right relationship with the Earth, in right timing with the stars and heavens, and with sacred purpose for the spirits of the Andes.

CEKE LINES

Energetic Currents of the Earth

When we look back at ancient civilizations, what we see throughout all cultures is that they had a deep knowledge of the Earth as a living being. The ancients could connect with the Earth and commune with the Earth, and by doing so they were able to live in harmony with the Earth in all of her seasons and with all of her elements.

Just as our physical bodies have veins of blood running rivers of life to all of our organs and tissues, keeping them alive with a source of life and energy, the Earth also has currents and veins of energy moving through her rivers, oceans, mountains, forests, and deserts. These rivers of energy in the Earth are known as meridians, ley lines, and/or dragon lines.

When different ley lines, or energetic currents in the Earth, meet and come together, they create a point of power. In each culture around the world, wise men and women knew how to follow the Earth's energetic currents, and because of this ability, they were able to locate and establish different points of power for their region and community. These wise men and women sanctioned these points of power by building temples and sacred sites on them. This enabled the channeling of energy from the Earth to the indigenous communities, the tribe, and the world.

In England our Celtic ancestors built Stonehenge and aligned this site to the energies of the winter and summer solstices. The ancient Egyptians built the great pyramids on the Giza Plateau and aligned these monolithic stone structures to the celestial bodies above. Like these ancient cultures around the world, the Inca were also in tune with the movements and currents of the Earth and her energies, for they had a deep knowledge and understanding that the Earth was a living being, an entity which we humans, and all of life, are a part of.

Throughout the Andean mountain range we can find the ancient ruins and temples of the Incan Empire, which were aligned to the seasons of the Earth, the fluctuations of the heavenly bodies above, and different animals found on their sacred lands.

These temples not only channeled the energies of the Great Above (the energies of the stars and heavens) and the Great Below (the energies of the Earth and this physical dimension), they also channeled the energies of the Great Within—the energies of the different ley lines coursing through the core of Pachamama.

In the ancient civilizations of the Andes we can find a shared understanding and body of knowledge pertaining to what are referred to as *ceke* lines. Ceke lines are synonymous with ley lines. The people of the Andes viewed each ceke line, or ley line, as corresponding to one of three different energetic categories. These three categories are known as Kollana, Payan, and Kayao.

The Three Ceke Lines and Their Energetic Frequencies

Below is a list of the three types of ceke lines classified by the ancient civilizations of the Andes. While each of these lines corresponded with a specific energy found coursing through the Earth, each of these ceke lines also aligns with one of the three pachas of the Andean cosmology—the Ukhu Pacha, the Kay Pacha, and the Hanan Pacha. As the ancient Inca built their temples upon these different places of power, they aligned them to the energies of the earth and the heavens, once again honoring the ancient spiritual maxim "As above, so below."

+ **Kollana:** Kollana is the ceke line that carries the frequency of timelessness and space outside of our physical dimension. Kollana is aligned with Condor and the Hanan Pacha of the Andean cosmology, and it channels the frequency of the Great Above through the core of Earth. This ceke line vibrates beyond time and space, and it has a connection to the stars, heavens, and the celestial bodies of Source.

+ **Payan:** This ceke line channels the frequency of time and space in physical reality. Payan is the ley line of 3D reality. In the Andean cosmology, the payan ceke line corresponds to the Kay Pacha and Puma. This line vibrates to the frequency of our physical dimension.

+ **Kayo:** The ceke lines known as kayo also carry the frequency of our space and time. The energies of these ley lines vibrate and align with Serpent and the Ukhu Pacha, and they channel the energy of our instinctual drives, desires, and needs.

As noted earlier, when two or more of these lines intersected and came together the people of the Andes would build their temples and sacred places of power there. Much as the Himalayan Mountains function as antennas of the masculine polarity and the Andes Mountains function as an antennas of the feminine polarity, these different temples channeled the energies coming from the Earth through these different ceke lines and they would also pull down the energies of the heavens, thereby dispersing these celestial energies upon Earth.

When the Serpent of Light (the energy or kundalini of planet Earth) moved from the Himalayan Mountains and situated itself beneath the Andes, it awakened the energies of these ceke lines and the ancient Incan temples. The Serpent of Light brought more chi, or life-force energy, to these sites and to this ancient culture once again.

When we are able to visit these temples and cities today, and we are aware of the original intention (or blueprint) behind each of these timeless constructions, we are able to see into them much more than the average tourist can. When we can connect with the original intention of a site, we can connect with the energies—the ancient magic of the Inca—and directly experience the shamanic wisdom found in this region of the world.

EACH SITE CALLS TO EACH OF US DIFFERENTLY

I have been in many sacred sites in Cuzco, the Sacred Valley, Machu Picchu, North and South Peru, and around Lima. What I have discovered in my countless journeys to Peru throughout these past three decades is that these temples, sacred sites, and cities speak differently to each of us, and all who are called to take a journey to Peru discover for themselves a place of power in these sacred lands.

My power place is Machu Picchu, but a lot of people who journey with me discover that their power place is Sacsayhuamán. Others choose Moray, or Ollantaytambo, or rather they are chosen by the sites themselves. So we all have a special connection to one of these sites. We find that one of these places of power touches us in some way different than others. As we walk through it and connect with the mysteries stored at this specific point of power, we receive an activation or an awakening. Perhaps we remember being in these same places several lifetimes ago.

Whether we find ourselves remembering past lives, receiving activations within ourselves, or experiencing shamanic transformation and healing—each of these sites and temples carries a vibration and an energy that influences us all in some way. When we undergo a journey to Peru and we walk this land with open hearts and sacred intention, we open the doors (and ourselves) to magic, and our lives change.

There is a profound medicine that is produced when we experience heartfelt connections with the local inhabitants of a different culture—with one another and with the land. We remember that we truly are connected to everyone and everything. We all share the same breath, the same heartbeat, and we all smile in the same language. When we journey to Peru or another ancient site on our planet, we remember and experience what the ancients have been teaching for millennia—we are all connected; we are all related.

This recollection will inform you when you visit the power places of Peru. Let's examine some of them more closely now.

TIWANAKU

Tiwanaku is the most ancient city in the Andean Mountains. Located in western Bolivia near Lake Titicaca, Tiwanaku is an archaeological site of great mystery. Full of relics from an unknown origin and from an unknown age, Tiwanaku is a city from our distant past, but no one seems to know just how distant. To the ancient Inca, Tiwanaku was believed to be the origin of all Creation.

Tiwanaku was revered as the "navel at the center." *Tiwanaku* also translates to mean "receiver" and "transmitter." This site is believed to be a temple made by magicians and scientists, and the symbols and glyphs throughout it are said to record the history of the star people living on Earth. Tiwanaku and the sacred monuments in this site are utilized for communication with other levels, dimensions, and realities.

As one of the greatest and largest archaeological sites in South

America, Tiwanaku is home to megalithic stone monuments and energetic portals of otherworldly origins. In the central plaza of Tiwanaku there are many stones that record significant celestial events that occurred at least fifteen thousand years ago. Tiwanaku is also home to the Gate of the Sun and Kalasasaya.

The Gate of the Sun

The Gate of the Sun is a stone monument that roughly measures ten feet tall by thirteen feet wide. This ancient gateway is a single stone creation carved with glyphs and symbols that are documented to predate the Inca. This relic contains the secret knowledge of otherworldly masters that is still waiting to be translated and decoded.

In his book *The Calendar of Tiahuanaco* Professor Hans Schindler-Bellamy interprets the symbols on the Gate of the Sun and shares that this site was used as a calendar for a civilization that existed more than twelve thousand years ago. According to his interpretation and translation, this civilization lived on Earth at a time when Earth had a different solar orbit, axial tilt, and even a different moon than what our planet has today. This information suggests that the sites and temples of Tiwanaku were able to access knowledge from different realities and dimensions of existence.

Most of Tiwanaku was destroyed by an immense cataclysm. The Gate of the Sun was one of the few constructions that survived that catastrophe. After the cataclysm, the essence of Tiwanaku changed and it became the center of another culture. This culture erected Kalasasaya, a courtyard of stones carefully placed to establish a new calendar of time. This calendar reflects the transition of the Earth as it made its way into a sun cycle of 365 days in a year.

We know that the Earth has had a long history, with many civilizations, some of them being highly advanced societies that came and went, leaving their legacy of consciousness and high technology in the form of megalithic constructions all around the world. The wisdom within these structures can still be deciphered in our present day by those with an open mind.

SHAMANIC JOURNEY

TO TIWANAKU

Guided by Vera Lopez

Take a deep breath, exhale fully, and relax your body. Take another deep breath, exhale fully, and close your eyes. It is now time to travel inside that space within the heart—we know this space to be sacred, and when we enter the "tiny space" of the heart, we are able to experience everything and nothing, all at the same time. This space is a portal throughout time and across space, and we can use this space to travel between the worlds and galaxies within all universes.

Take a moment to breathe into these energies, and find this liminal space in your own heart. Within this space, set your intention to travel to Lake Titicaca—the sacred lake that separates Peru and Bolivia. This body of water was sacred to the ancient Inca, and the ancients revered this lake as being the creative force of life itself.

So see yourself standing upon the shores of Lake Titicaca—see yourself there within your mind's eye, and be there now.

This holy water shimmers before you as if a million stars floated upon its surface. Feel into the essence of this lake and connect to the Apus residing within its depths. Lake Titicaca is a divine portal of feminine energy, and it is believed that those who have the ears to hear and the eyes to see can use this portal to travel back to Tiwanaku. Walk along the shores of Lake Titicaca and allow Tiwanaku, the sacred site, to find and part the veils before you—allowing you to travel once again throughout time and space back to the land where everything began.

As you travel back in time thousands of years to this beautiful empire, you are guided to the sacred temples once built by an advanced civilization within a time outside of time. You walk through the beautiful complex of temples and see stone walls within stone walls, altars, and other meaningful sacred places that hold mysteries and knowledge from the ancient world. Breathing deeply, you continue to journey until you come across a gateway before you. Within your heart space, you know that this gateway is the Gate of the Sun—the portal to the dimensions of light.

You move toward it and, standing underneath the arch, open your arms and breathe deeply, inviting the ancient wisdom of Viracocha—the creator god of the universe in the Andean cosmology—to touch your heart and your mind so that you may receive the activations found with the holy and sacred library of souls.

Within your mind's eye you begin to see flashes of different lifetimes and you recognize yourself within these different times, spaces, and dimensions—you find yourself manifested within your previous and future life expressions, receiving and accessing the wisdom found within each of your different projections. In all of these different personalities and incarnations, you know that you have played many different roles and have developed much wisdom in order to be where you are at this present moment. These experiences—this information and wisdom—is poignant for your present day and age, especially as we collectively transition into the Age of Aquarius where a new consciousness is rising. All of these experiences, all of these incarnations—experienced by your soul and by the souls of others—form the foundation for this new consciousness, this new aeon of unified wisdom.

Spend some more time within the portal of the archway, and allow the cosmic consciousness that transcends time and space to share with you a message or a vision—some piece of medicine or insight that is timely for you and your present-day life. Allow what comes to come, and do not judge what you see, feel, hear, or experience but trust it as stemming from that part of you that is deeply connected to the One.

Allow this vision to feel each cell of your body with life-force energy and potential, and feel yourself begin to let go of all that once restricted your soul, your spirit, and your truth. Stand within this archway—the Gate of the Sun—filled with your greatest potential and your greatest consciousness.

Breathe into this connection and give thanks for this moment, for this wisdom, and for this experience. Gather up bits and pieces of your journey and tuck them within your heart space.

As you step out of the portal the energetics and feelings of this transmission continue to reside within and fill your body. You give thanks to this portal and to the sacred site of Tiwanaku.

And once again, bring your awareness to that tiny space within your heart. Breathe into that vast space and allow it to expand even more. Then step inside your sacred space of the heart and allow it to transport you back into your present time, space, and dimension. Feeling yourself return to your body, breathe deeply and exhale fully. Wiggle your fingers and your toes, gently stretch and move, and when you feel ready, open your eyes.

Take some time to journal about your journey and record your experience.

PARACAS

Geographically, Paracas is a peninsula that extends off the southern coast of Peru. To the ancient Inca, Paracas was revered as the landing place of the gods. This ancient site is well-known for its large prehistoric geoglyph that is engraved on the northern face of the peninsula. This six-hundred-foot-tall geoglyph has been dated to 200 BCE, although many archaeologists believe that its existence stems back much further in history.

The design of the geoglyph can be described as having a foundational single stem, which then divides into three smaller branches, and each of these branches extends out again. Some have equated this design with that of a "candelabra," making this site known today as the Paracas Candelabra. This site has been referred to as the "tree of knowledge," although its actual purpose remains a mystery to date.

When we look at a map, we can see that Paracas, Tiwanaku, and Cuzco all align together to form a triangle; both Paracas and Tiwanaku are eleven hundred miles from Cuzco. This observation is interesting to consider, especially since each of these three sites share a common lore and mythology in the cosmology of the Andes. Each of these sites is considered to be the arrival or landing place of the gods, and they are each believed to hold an immense amount of ancient knowledge and wisdom from divine dimensions.

Over the past three decades I have facilitated many shamanic and spiritual journeys to Peru. In so doing, not only have I witnessed these powerful portals of the Incan Empire channel their transformational energy as they did once before in the time of the Inca, but I have also witnessed that these sacred temples are beginning to call spiritual seekers to them. These spiritual seekers are traveling from all over the world to experience and connect with the ancient sites of the Andes. And whether or not these journeyers are conscious of the spiritual energies channeled by these temples, I know and trust that the spirits of Peru have called them to its sacred land.

CUZCO

Navel of the Earth

THERE ARE A FEW LEGENDS of how Cuzco came to be. One of the most recognized myths is that after the cataclysm, Viracocha—the creator god of the Inca—came down in the manifestation of a man and a woman—a mystical couple named Manco Capac and Mama Ocllo. It is believed that this couple emerged from the waters of Lake Titicaca and their purpose was to find the new center of the world. Legends share that this couple journeyed across the lands of South America, walking with a staff of power and light. As Manco Capac and Mama Ocllo came upon the land of Cuzco, they could feel its holy energy and power. Together, they pierced the ground with their staff and declared that this point of power would be the new heart of their civilization. Thus the capital of the Incan Empire was born.

The Inca were deeply spiritual people—they lived their lives in right relationship and with right action with the world and elements around them. *Cuzco* derives from the Quechua word *quosco,* which means "center" or "navel of the world." To the Inca, Cuzco was the center of their empire, Tawantinsuyu—the Empire of the Four Directions. The city of Cuzco was built in the shape of a puma with a falcon's head. Even though Condor holds a much larger status within the Andean cosmology, the falcon and its energies are represented in one of the most significant temples of this region, Sacsayhuamán, which is located a couple of miles outside of the city of Cuzco.

CORICANCHA

Within the center of Cuzco was the Coricancha—the spiritual heart of the Incan Empire. To the ancient Inca, Coricancha was known as the "heart of the Puma" as, again, Cuzco was designed in the shape of a puma's body. Coricancha was not only the central point of all spiritual and ceremonial celebrations in Cuzco and the Incan Empire, it was also believed to be the centralized point for the ceke system—the ley line system of the Andes. The Incan temples and places of power were all built in alignment with the Coricancha.

This central point of power—the Coricancha—was constructed in alignment with the heavens of the Great Above. Anchoring these celestial energies, the Coricancha was designed and built as having four temples and a central plaza. Each of these four temples was aligned and sanctioned to the high gods and powers of sky: Inti (the god of the sun), Mama Killa (the goddess of the moon), Chasca (the star beings), and Illapa (the rainbow spirit).

According to Ed Krupp, author of *Echoes of the Ancient Skies: The Astronomy of Lost Civilizations*, "The Inca built the Coricancha at the confluence because that place represented terrestrially the organizing pivot of heaven." Intentionally placed and aligned within the heart of Cuzco—the capital of the Incan Empire—these four temples channeled and honored these celestial energies and influences. They generated powerful, divine forces throughout the ceke lines within the Earth to their other temples and power sites throughout the Tawantinsuyu.

SHAMANIC JOURNEY

TO CUZCO

Guided by Vera Lopez

Take a deep breath and exhale fully. Breathe deeply into your body and exhale fully. Closing your eyes, I invite you to drop deep into your own body and connect to the wisdom within. Your body, your mind, and your spirit create a powerful vehicle for you to travel in. When you invoke the power of your intention and unify it with your imagination, you can journey anywhere throughout time and space.

With this knowledge, I invite you to breathe deeply and bring your attention to your pineal gland. Imagine a luminous marble of light glowing within the center of your pineal gland—like a ball of light—floating and activating your special gifts of vision, insight, and intuition. This marble of light grows and expands and drops down into your own heart center, where it expands the loving consciousness within you. This light descends down from your heart into your navel—your solar plexus energy center. Within this energy center, the light grows even larger and empowers your "gut wisdom," the sun within you.

From this place where your pineal gland, heart center, and solar plexus are awakened and activated, you take your journey—journeying all the way to Cuzco—the capital of the Incan Empire; it is also believed to be the Navel of the Earth. You look around Cuzco and see the holy mountains—the Andes Mountains—off in the near distance. As you stand within this place of power—this ancient city of alchemy and higher vibration—you connect with the energies of the Andes and feel into them. These mountains are antennas, and they pull down the frequencies of the divine feminine rays of light and disperse them throughout the world.

You turn and look at the city around you and find that you are standing in a beautiful temple. The ancient Inca believed Cuzco to be the Temple of the Sun, and they called this power place the Coricancha. The Coricancha is a beautiful temple made of gold and it carries the high frequencies of light.

You walk around the temple of gold and find yourself facing an ancient disk made of gold and engraved with different symbols. This is the sun disk of Mu—the ancient civilization that predates Lemuria and Atlantis. You stare at this powerful item of power, and the symbols and engravings upon it begin to move and dance in front of you—creating a fusion of vibration and frequency that invite you to receive the wisdom, the light, and the potential of enlightenment.

Breathe into these timeless energies and allow them to fill your own spirit, your own mind, and your own body. Feel yourself connect to these energies and allow these energies to connect to you. Be present with the exchange that occurs when you give and receive simultaneously.

Breathing deeply, you are aware that within this moment you are experiencing the highest manifestation of ayni—the law of reciprocity. Stay in this moment and be as a disciple would be with a teacher—emmeshed in the Divine within and the Divine without. Allow this circuit of transformative energy to flow back and forth between your own body, mind, and spirit, and the ancient sun disk of Mu.

And as you continue to breathe and ground in this powerful exchange, the sun disk before you begins to melt—dispersing its powerful, alchemical gold energy across the planet; blessing all kingdoms, all people, all places, and all beings with this energy of transmutation and rebirth. This golden light fills the planet and touches all life, then radiates throughout the cosmos—ushering in the new consciousness of humanity. Within this vision within a vision, you see how all kingdoms, all people, and all living beings everywhere thrive with life-force energy and how this infusion of golden light expands the heart-minds of everything and everyone it touches.

This planetary alchemical blessing renews our beloved Pachamama, and through this renewal, all life on Earth and throughout the cosmos is renewed as well. This energy of renewal guides you to be one with everything and one with Source energy. Breathe into this connection and this greater consciousness and allow it to fill and flow throughout your body.

After a while, you take a deep breath in through your nose and exhale through your mouth. And within your vision-within-a-vision, the golden light comes back into the formation of a sun disk in front of you—engraved with all of its designs and symbols, vibrating at a high frequency.

You smile looking at the disk and you know that—even within your mind's eye—the planet and the world around you received a powerful alchemical blessing of rebirth, renewal, and transmutation.

This is the blessing of Coricancha—the Temple of the Sun within the Navel of the Earth. This is the magic of Cuzco, and you can return here and perform this alchemical magic anytime you desire. For now it's time to return to your physical body, in your present time, space, and dimension.

So take a deep breath and exhale fully, and allow yourself to travel back into your physical body now. Breathing in and breathing out, return to your body with full awareness of your divine connection and give thanks for the blessings of light and rebirth you received on this journey. Wiggle your fingers and your toes, breathing deeply—and when you feel ready, open your eyes.

SACSAYHUAMÁN

The fortress of Sacsayhuamán is just north of Cuzco, the capital of the Incan Empire. *Sacsayhuamán* in Quechua means "falcon" or "hawk." Sacsayhuamán is famed for its remarkable, large, dry-stone walls— boulders carefully cut to fit together tightly without mortar. The stones used in the construction of the terraces at Sacsayhuamán weigh up to two hundred tons and are among the largest stones used in any temple found in pre-Hispanic America. In addition to their vast weight and size, each of these stones fit together with such precision and cohesiveness that not even a piece of paper can fit between them. This precision, combined with the rounded corners of the blocks, the variety of their interlocking shapes, and the way the walls lean inward have puzzled scientists for decades.

To understand Sacsayhuamán's importance, we have to go back to a time before the Inca. According to water erosion records, archaeologists know that Sacsayhuamán was built prior to the last ice age, which means that this site was only discovered by the Inca, not constructed by them. The Incan civilization began in Cuzco around 1200 CE with the very first Inca: Manco Capac and Mama Ocllo. Elaborating greatly on previous life in Cuzco, the Inca built what we now know as Cuzco city. It was divided into two sectors, the *urin* and *hanan,* each arranged to include two of the four provinces (also known as suyus, representing the northwest, northeast, southwest, and southeast quarters).

After this initial foundation of Cuzco, the Incan city went into a second period of growth around 1400. Archaeological evidence suggests gradual growth before the rule of Pachacuti, however the Incan history of Cuzco states that King Pachacuti led this expansive phase. It was the start of his transformation of Cuzco from sleepy city-state to the vast empire of Tawantinsuyu. Many believed the new layout of the city was planned as an effigy, for as we have learned, it was distinctively in the shape of a puma, a sacred animal in Incan culture. The fortress of Sacsayhuamán formed the head, the plaza of Huacaypata the navel, and the converging Huatanay and Tullumayo Rivers the tail.

Sacsayhuamán was the center where great ceremonial gatherings took place, primarily seasonal celebrations and initiatory processes for Incan boys. There is a specific sector in Sacsayhuamán designated for the initiatory process. These sections of the temple are carved with ancient mysteries, and they are believed to be directly connected to the gods.

Even today, Peruvians use Sacsayhuamán to celebrate Inti Raymi, the Incan Sun Festival.

ABOUT INTI RAYMI
The Incan Sun Festival

Inti Raymi, or the Incan Sun Festival, was the most important religious ceremony of the Incan Empire in honor of the sun god (Inti). Inti Raymi is celebrated on the shortest day of the year in terms of the time between sunrise and sunset (winter solstice). At Inti Raymi the Inca, the priests, and all the people pay homage to the sun god.

Inti Raymi was the most important festival in the time of the Inca. It not only held religious and ceremonial importance but also had social and political elements as well, thus making it a celebrated and honored festival throughout the whole of Tawantinsuyu.

After the Spanish conquest in 1532, the Catholic Church suppressed the ceremony, and the Andean society that had celebrated this festivity to the sun was dismembered, given that the celebration of the Catholic Saint James had superseded it. The festival of Inti Raymi was forgotten and not celebrated again until 1944 when a group of intellectuals and artists from Cuzco headed by Cuzco historian Humberto

Vidal Unda decided to recover the historical Inti Raymi and to present it as a show of a theatrical type dedicated to the whole population of Cuzco. From then on, it has been represented every year, getting rich and continuing to evolve.

One of my most magical moments in Peru was at my first Inti Raymi. To the Inca, Inti Raymi is the shortest day of the year and the longest night. The Inca used this time to pray and honor the sun god, Inti. Villages and tribes from all over the Empire of the Four Directions would gather together in Cuzco and they would each bring the best of the best from their villages—the best dancers, the best stones, the best dancers and food—whatever they considered the best of their village was brought to the ceremonial grounds in Cuzco. In the days of the Inca, the ceremonial grounds would be filled with dancers, musicians, and priests offering their prayers to welcome back the sun.

My first Inti Raymi was a very cold day in Cuzco. There was a sort of mist in the air and the sky was filled with dark silver clouds. What I remember most about this day was the end of the Inti Raymi ceremony. Nowadays, actors and dancers are chosen to reenact the roles of the ancient's festival, and to be chosen is regarded as a great honor.

Toward the end of this ceremony, the Inca stands in the center of the ceremonial grounds and speaks to Inti, the sun god. When the man playing the role of the Inca stood in the center and spoke his prayers of power, welcoming the sun back to life, you could feel his devotion in his words. He was speaking in Quechua with such passion from his heart as he was offering gratitude to the sun. As he offered his invocations to Inti—calling the sun god forth and welcoming him back to life—the clouds opened up at this exact moment and a beam of light shone down upon the Incan priest invoking Inti in the center of the ceremony. Shortly after this, a rainbow appeared over the entire ceremony.

This is one of my most magical stories of Peru because it demonstrates how, when you speak to nature with an active munay, nature listens and responds. At this moment it was clear to me that Inti had heard this man's words and could feel the munay in this man's prayers.

This Inti Raymi memory reminds me that nature is always listening and responding to us.

Today, Cuzco is alive with spiritual energy, mysticism, and mysteries. You will know you are in Cuzco when you arrive at the airport—you will see a display of iconic pictures and colors, hear a variety of music, and you will be surrounded by lots of backpackers and tourists. Leaving the airport, you will see a series of markets. In these markets, the local women are selling alpacas, coca-leaf candy, and the common trinkets that are found throughout most markets in Peru. Moving further, into the heart of Cuzco, you will see the streets are filled with a wide range of locals and tourists from all over the world.

Cuzco hosts a plethora of healing centers that offer yoga, meditation, sound healing, and even ayahuasca ceremonies. A large portion of the people who are drawn to Cuzco are called to this city to experience deeper levels of healing and inner work.

In the time of the Inca, Cuzco served as the center point of the entire Incan Empire. Today its mission and spiritual purpose is to assist all those who are called to experience the ancient mysticism of Peru and the Inca. While it is no longer the center of the Tawantinsuyu, Cuzco still anchors an enormous vibration of energy and offers a transmission of power to all those who yearn to know more about this ancient city and the magic that it holds.

MORAY

Womb of the Inca

TUCKED IN THE OUTSKIRTS OF CUZCO are the ancient Incan ruins of Moray. Moray is a set of circular terraces that descend down into the Earth. The Inca used these terraces as a laboratory where they experimented with the growth of different crops and plant life. Moray holds the energy of life, of birth, and of creation.

The shamanic initiation of Moray focuses on connecting to the womb of Mother Earth. With each layer and terrace, we descend closer and closer to the Navel of the Earth and form a direct connection with Pachamama—the Divine Mother who gave birth to all things.

In the Andean tradition, Pachamama is not just the Earth Mother, she is the Cosmic Mother—the creatrix of life itself. She holds the secrets and mysteries to life, death, and rebirth and she supports us through each of these shamanic initiations. At Moray, seekers are able to connect with Pachamama and descend down into her core, allowing themselves to be held and then reborn from the Great Mother's womb.

As seekers journey down into the terraces, they are able to remember their own sacred relationship with their own birth mother. During their journey, many seekers recall experiences that occurred in the womb, and they are able to heal any trauma from their birth process and/or their relationship with their birth mother.

For the ancients, Moray was the womb of the Earth as manifested by the circular terraces. Here, the initiates and shamans were able to connect to the fertility of the Earth's womb. Here they were able to plant their dreams, seed their visions for the future, and feel the energy of life emerging from their own core and being. Moray gifted the ancient shamans with the energies of fertility and creation, and it continues to share these gifts with visiting seekers today.

Regardless of the specific experience, Moray is change. Embedded within these ancient ruins is an initiation of birth and creation. As we journey throughout these ancient stone terraces, we remember the oneness that is created when duality merges with itself. At Moray, we remember that we are all connected through the breath, and we remember that through the initiations of birth, life, and death we are all held by the Pachamama—the Great Mother of all that is.

SHAMANIC JOURNEY
TO MORAY
Guided by Vera Lopez

Take a deep breath—inhale fully through your nose and exhale through your mouth. Breathe in once more, exhale fully, and close your eyes. In your mind's eye envision a golden orb of light surrounding your physical body. This golden light will serve as your body's psychic protection while you journey between the worlds of space and time.

Taking another deep breath in, I invite you to let your spirit journey up and out of your body, and feel your spirit soar into the sky above you. It innately knows how to travel between the worlds, and as you continue to fly through the sky above you, you travel to the land of Peru and the Sacred Valley of the Inca. Gently descending into the Sacred Valley, you land softly on the ground.

Before you is the ancient Temple of Moray. You walk to the edge of the cliff and peer down below you and see that within Moray there are eight terraces going down deep into the Earth. These terraces have generated powerful energy for centuries, for Moray is a vortex of healing energy. The ancient Inca used this ancient temple as a healing vortex into the womb of Pachamama—Mother Earth.

Take a deep breath and prepare yourself to enter this vortex of energy. You begin your journey down into the womb of Mother Earth. Terrace by terrace you descend deeper and deeper into the Earth—this holy, living vessel of life.

As you journey throughout the terraces, you notice different herbs and plants on each one. You intuitively know that these herbs are all healing plants, and you know that they were used as medicine by the ancient Inca.

Being present to yourself, and going deeper into your conscious- ness, you continue to journey down each terrace, into this vortex, and feel your connection with Pachamama—Mother Earth. You know that as you journey down into the womb of Mother Earth you are also returning back into the womb of your own mother—the place where you were once a seed, where the seeds of all future potential and life reside.

Take a deep breath in and settle your spirit within the energies of the womb. Connect with the womb of your own mother and the womb of Mother Earth. Within this space, look within your own heart and see where you are wounded.

Where do you hold pain, grief, sorrow, loss, and disappointment? What areas of your own life feel disconnected from life, love, and the nurturing energies of the Great Mother?

Where is your soul still bleeding?

Moray is a powerful place of healing, a power center where we can activate and remember the seeds of forgiveness and love that still, despite everything, reside within us. Knowing that you are a whole and complete being, bring these areas of your life where you feel pain, bro- ken, and disconnected into this healing energy.

Bring the people, places, and things that have harmed you, and that you have harmed, into this powerful womb of Moray and allow all of these experiences to be held within this ancient energy field.

The journey down into Moray is also a journey down into your own heart where you can find the love and forgiveness you need to set your- self free from the wounds and pains of your past. If you have hurt others, invite their spirits forward and ask forgiveness. If you have been hurt by others, invite their spirits to these medicine circles, and forgive them for the pain and hurt they inflicted upon you.

Breathe into your own heart space and feel yourself held in the ancient womb of Mother Earth. Know that your ability to forgive and be forgiven is the pathway to freedom for your soul.

As you free yourself from the pains of the past, you notice that you are now standing in the center of Moray—the deepest point in the womb of Pachamama. Within this center, you feel your spirit completely liberated. You are no longer a prisoner of the stories of your past—you are free.

Moray stands for change—the change that comes from transformation. This change is not from what is different or what separates us as individuals. Rather it represents what has been transmuted and what can be rebirthed. As you stand here within the center depths of Moray, you have been reborn through the healing energies of love and forgiveness. Feel yourself, your heart, and your spirit renewed by these ancient energies.

Taking a piece of hair from your head, leave it as an offering of thanks and gratitude to this ancient place of medicine; leave it as an offering to the Great Mother—Pachamama.

Once you feel complete, begin your journey back up the terraces of Moray—carrying with you the freedom and joy in your heart. As you climb each terrace, feel yourself coming back to your consciousness. As you step out of Moray, you jump up into the air and your spirit begins to fly once again—feeling whole and free.

Allow your spirit to fly back into this time and space, finding your body surrounded by the golden light of protection. Your spirit enters your body and you take a deep breath in through your nose and out through your mouth. You breathe in and give gratitude for your imagination and your deep sense of connecting to an experience outside of time and space.

Take a moment to wiggle your fingers and toes, and when you feel ready, open your eyes. Journal your experience and integrate your journey.

OLLANTAYTAMBO

House of the Dawn

OLLANTAYTAMBO IS A BEAUTIFUL TOWN that preserves the life of the ancient Inca. Within every structure, upon every street, and held within every wall resides the heart and spirit of the Inca. Even within our modern age, seekers can immerse themselves in the lifestyle of this ancient civilization when they journey to Ollantaytambo.

The Incan fortress was built around the middle of the fifteenth century, and it is the second most well-preserved ruin in Peru. It was named after the warrior Ollanta, whose family, the Anta, were lords of the area. The Anta were related to the royal Incan line, but not full-blooded royalty themselves.

Unfortunately for him, Ollanta fell in love with the daughter of the Sapa (high) Inca of the time. Ollanta was a noble but not a "true" Inca, thus the love affair between Ollanta and the Sapa's daughter was forbidden.

One day, the royal sons of the Sapa Inca were kidnapped and taken by the Chanka People—inhabitants of the Apurimac region near Cuzco. The legend has it that it was Ollanta who rescued the Sapa's sons from the Chanka people and brought them back home to their village. Through his heroic acts, Ollanta gained the acceptance and approval of the Sapa Inca, and he was allowed to love and marry the Sapa's daughter.

This story of overcoming all obstacles in pursuit of love encapsulates the energy of Ollantaytambo and its most recognized temple, the Temple of the Sun, which is more commonly known as the Lemurian

Temple of Love. This temple is built upon a high mountain that is comprised of pink and green granite and an array of other minerals. The only pathway and entrance into this temple is to climb a series of serpentine staircases that weave up and through the many terraces and platforms of this ancient site.

Standing at the top of the terraces and staircases is a gigantic structure comprised of six massive pink walls. Each of these monolithic pink stones is a portal—a doorway into another time, space, and/or dimension, and encoded within each of these stones are special frequencies and ancient transmissions programed at a time long before our own.

Edgar Elorrieta Salazar shares in his book *Cusco and the Sacred Valley of Peru* that Ollantaytambo is also known as Pacaritanpu, which is Quechua for "House of the Dawn" or "House of Windows." Another chronicler by the name of Joan de Santa Cruz Pachacuti shares cultural lore and legend about Ollantaytambo by writing: "the staff left by Viracochan (Tunupa) was transmuted to gold at the moment when one of the descendants of the Tambo lord was born. He took the name of Manco Capac and taking up the staff of gold, he directed his steps to the highest parts of a mountainous land where he founded the city of Cusco" (see Foerster, *Lost Ancient Technology of Peru and Bolivia*).

What Pachacuti is suggesting in his writing is that the first Inca, Manco Capac, did not come from Tiwanaku as the most widely accepted lore and legend states. Pachacuti is suggesting that the birthplace of the Inca is Ollantaytambo. While this has not been documented as fact, it would mean that—as in all oral traditions—the name "House of the Dawn" has a double meaning: a specific time of morning and the "dawning," or origin, of the Inca civilization.

Adjacent to the Temple of the Sun is the mountain Pinkuylluna. Shaped within the matrix of this mountain is the face of Viracocha, the Incan god of Creation. Viracocha's face stares directly upon the Temple of the Sun, and it can be seen anywhere within Ollantaytambo. This sacred rock formation, representing the face of the Creator, aligns perfectly with the Pleiades constellation—reminding the Incan people and the modern-day seekers of their ancient lineage with the stars.

Ollantaytambo, the Temple of the Sun (the Lemurian Temple of

Love), and the stone face of Viracocha all call seekers to step onto the serpentine staircase and shed any blockages held within their heart space, encouraging them to breathe and expand their heart field as they climb to the top of the temple. Once seekers are at the top, they connect with the six pink stones. Here, transmissions of higher love and wisdom permeate their energetic field—supporting seekers as they connect to the bigger picture held in their heart's space and they remember their lineage with the stars.

SHAMANIC JOURNEY
TO OLLANTAYTAMBO
Guided by Vera Lopez

Take a deep breath—inhale fully through your nose and exhale through your mouth. Breathe in once more, exhale fully, and close your eyes. In your mind's eye envision a golden orb of light surrounding your physical body. This golden light will serve as your body's psychic protection while you journey between the worlds of space and time.

You find yourself journeying to the Andes Mountains, to the sacred and ancient site of Ollantaytambo. The hour is dawn, and you are held between the light and the dark. You look before you and see the greatest staircase of ancient stones ahead of you. Gazing at the top of these steps you see a temple encased by the mists of the mountains. Intuitively you know that there are ancient Lemurian sages waiting for you in this temple, and is time for you to begin your journey up to the Temple of Love, also known as the Temple of the Sun.

You start your pilgrimage walking gently with beauty, kindness, and peace. These steps were made by wise ones who knew that to rise to consciousness we must move forward and upward. So you continue your journey, rising within consciousness, step by step, listening to the silence whispering within your soul, inviting you to breathe deeply into your heart.

Take a deep breath and open your heart center. Allow your heart center to light up, bright like the sun above you. Breathing deeply again, open and illuminate your power center and then your third eye. Allow the light of these energy centers to guide you forward along your journey to the great sages of the Lemurian Council.

As you climb, you realize that these ancient steps are made out of serpentine stone, and they hold the power to cleanse and remove blockages from your energy body. You climb higher and higher, allowing your energy and auric fields to become clearer, lighter, and brighter.

Finally reaching the top of the stairs, you are greeted by the Lemurian sages who welcome and embrace you. As you stand in their presence you telepathically receive images in your mind and heart. These images are gifts from these sages, and they are your tools of power. Take a moment to connect to their images in your mind and heart, and discover what gifts these Lemurian sages are sharing with you.

The journey to the Temple of Ollantaytambo—the Lemurian Temple of Love—is a holy pilgrimage. This journey is an ancient initiation that calls you forth to step into and embody your own priesthood and/or priestesshood. The gifts found in your mind and heart are your tools of power to carry out your specific ministry, your sacred calling and purpose.

The sages place you before six large stones. These stones are rose quartz and they radiate a pink glow in the sunlight. As you stand before these giant stones, you recognize that each of them is a portal of light. Feel into each of the different portals and see which doorway of light is calling to your heart today. Find your portal, approach it, and step through its luminous doorway.

You walk through this portal of light and you travel through dimensions, receiving downloads of information and insights that transcend time and space. Each piece of information and insight you receive is relevant to your evolutionary journey. Absorb what you are receiving, and know that you will always be able to access these portals of light and knowledge whenever you desire.

You can stay within this portal of light for as long as you like, and when you are complete with your journey, you can walk back through the stone doorways, illuminated in a pink and golden light, and you will find your spirit back in your physical body.

Once you return to your physical body, take a couple of deep breaths to fully ground from your experience. Wiggle your fingers and your toes, and when you feel ready, open your eyes. Take some time to process, journal, and reflect on your journey and integrate your experiences.

PISAC

The Seer's Chair

PISAC IS A VILLAGE SITUATED AT THE MOUTH of the Sacred Valley. About seventeen miles from Cuzco, Pisac is home to the iconic terrace gardens, which are just below the ancient ruin site of Inca Pisac. In the time of the Inca, Pisac was a key provider of the empire's agricultural needs. The terrace gardens, which are still in operation today, supplied the bulk of the crops for the surrounding villages and communities. Being in close proximity to Cuzco, Pisac functioned as a connecting village along the route of the Incan road.

Pisac translates to mean "partridge," which is a species of wood quails native to Peru. In fact, it is recorded that the layout of the terrace gardens was intentionally designed to reflect the pattern found on the partridge wing feathers. Pisac today is regularly visited by journeyers. Home to the best markets, Pisac has an entire square in which the villagers sell their crafts and creations.

Pisac maintains a strong connection to the physical realm with its terraced gardens and shopping markets. This Incan village also maintains a deep connection to the ancient shamanic mysteries of Peru. Pisac is seeded with a wisdom that comes from the stars and the heavens—the ancient origins of humanity.

▶▶◀◀

PISAC

Mysteries of the As Above, So Below

In mystery schools and spiritual traditions around the world, we find this shared principle of an ancient spiritual maxim, *As above, so below.* Each and every culture has mystics and wise ones who could look into the stars and heavens and obtain the wisdom being downloaded to humanity from the gods above. In the Christian tradition, we find writings that remind us that heaven is a place on earth. Biblical passages such as "On Earth as it is in Heaven" and the "Kingdom of God (Heaven) lives within" bring us back to this ancient spiritual maxim, reminding us that the events transpiring up above affect and influence the Earth below.

In indigenous cultures, we find a shared belief that human beings originated from the stars. Modern-day science and researchers are finding evidence that the same molecules and elements living in our bodies have trace amounts of particles that match the same make-up as molecules and elements found in space. We human beings are, as the late Carl Sagan would say, "star stuff."

The cosmos is our home, and the stars are our ancestry. Our great, great, great-grandparents—our original mothers and fathers—are found within the stars. The ancient Egyptians believed we originated from Sirius—the great Dog Star of the cosmos—and in the Andes Mountains of Peru, the Q'eros shamans believe that we all are direct descendants of the Pleiades—a constellation of seven sister stars, which happen to be one of the closest star systems to Earth. So when we say "as above, so below," what we (and the early mystics) are really saying is that when we look to the Great Above—the stars, planets, and heavens—we are really looking into our lineage for the wisdom and knowledge needed to live here on planet Earth—the Great Below.

This is where the sciences and studies of astrology and astronomy emerged from—this looking to the Above for guidance and wisdom for life here Below. For people who are of the Earth and in close relationship to Pachamama, like those living within the Andes Mountains of Peru, know and understand that in order to live upon our planet we must look to the stars.

In all indigenous cultures around the world we find that within the various tribes and communities there is always one sect or one person in the village who can read the stars. Whether they were called priests, shamans, seers, or astrologers, these wise men and women were important to the success and life of the whole village. Without these people connected to the wisdom of the Great Above—the stars and heavens—the villages, tribes, and communities would not know when to plant their seeds, harvest their crops, and prepare for the seasonal changes. These wise men and women knew how to read the maps of the Great Above, and through this information they were able to help navigate life here on Earth.

Established at an elevation of about ten thousand feet, the ruins of Pisac were once home to the ancient astrologers and seers of the Incan Empire. This community of wise seers studied the heavens above. Living at such high elevations, these wise ones were able to decipher and read the codes and messages being transmitted to planet Earth from the Hanan Pacha, or the Great Above.

The seers of Pisac, the ones who lived on top of the mountains, were responsible for reading the stars and communicating the planetary shifts and celestial movements to the agricultural village below. These seers also functioned as the priests and priestesses in that they remembered the ceremonies and rituals, and they knew when and how to honor the solstices and the equinoxes. By having an intimate relationship with the stars and the heavens above—the Hanan Pacha—the seers of Pisac were able to teach the villagers below how to live in right relationship with the Earth.

These seers shared one of the most shamanic mysteries living within our world—growing crops. In my opinion, nothing is more shamanic by definition than knowing how to put tiny seeds in the Earth, cover them with dirt, and nurture them into fruitful beings, becoming food for the tribe and the community. This shamanic wisdom is all divined by the wisdom found in the movement of the stars above.

How did these seers know how to read and follow the movement of the stars? Who showed them and nurtured them in these shamanic mysteries? Perhaps there is an ancient mystery school whose lineage goes back to our most our ancient roots—the stars above. Perhaps there are wise beings residing in the heavens—within the Great Star Nations. And as life on Earth was developing, these wise celestial beings showed our early ancestors on Earth how to read the maps of the universe so that they could understand and know when to plant the seeds, harvest the crops, and honor the solstices. Conceivably, this knowledge and wisdom has been shared and passed down generation after generation, and these mysteries are still alive today.

SHAMANIC JOURNEY
TO PISAC

Guided by Star Wolf

Pisac is the uniting place where the energies of the Great Above and the So Below come together in sacred union. The ancients believed that this region of Peru was the union place of Inti (the Andean sun god) and Pachamama (Mother Earth). They also believed the celestial energies and archetypes of the seven sister stars and Mama Killa—the moon— were easily accessible from this region's high mountaintops.

As you make the trek from the village to the ancient ruins, you climb from about six thousand feet to about ten thousand feet in elevation. This increase in elevation alone is quite a journey for the physical body. And as you walk the trail that winds and climbs along the edge of the mountains, you are able to view the village below as well as view the garden terraces where crops and sacred herbs grow nestled in the mountains.

For me, this is one of the most shamanic places of all of Peru, as it is a place where one can easily connect with the forces of the Great Above and the Great Below and bring them together within the Great Within.

When we make the pilgrimage to Pisac and visit the ancient ruins that overlook the village we are really taking a journey to connect with some of the oldest and wisest forces in our universe—the energies of the Great Star Nation and the energies of the Pachamama, or Mother Earth.

As you experience this journey below, I invite you to open up to the mysteries of these ancient and ever-present forces in nature. Listen to their wisdom and remember that these forces are your ancient ancestry—they reside within your blood, body, and breath—reminding you and encouraging you to fully embody the fullness of your soul and your shamanic spirit.

So create a comfortable place where you can experience this journey. Perhaps create an altar of your sacred objects—reminding you of your own shamanic consciousness. Once your sacred space is established and set up, I invite you to take about ten full and deep breaths, activating all the energy centers in your body. Continue to breathe deeply—inhaling through your nose and exhaling fully through your mouth—and close your eyes.

Relax your body as you breathe and open your heart to the energies of your own shamanic being, who is equipped to walk between the worlds—traversing the realms of the Great Above, the Great Below, the Light, the Dark and all those places in between.

In your mind's eye imagine yourself standing down by the river that runs through the Sacred Valley of Peru, giving life to the crops and the people who live in this region of land. As you stand here, feel your humble connection and your interconnection to the Earth itself—feeling your connection to the waters running before you, the ground beneath your feet, the sky above you, and the air you are breathing. You are connected to the Earth and you are a part of this sacred land.

Looking down the river, feel into the energy of the village downstream. See where the people live, where their markets are set up, and where the farmers care for and maintain their crops and livestock. This village is a real, earthy place, and you intuitively know that all those who live here share your connection to the Earth and the elements around you.

Imagine yourself in this village. What role do you play and how do you contribute to your community? Are you a farmer caring for the crops and the sacred herbs? Do you weave fabrics or make wool for clothing? What is your sacred niche within the village, and what actions do you fulfill on a mundane level to support the collective?

As you feel this connection, you find yourself being called to walk up the mountain—you are undergoing a vision quest for yourself and you are in search of how you can be a better human being at this time. You pack your bag—perhaps placing a flute and/or coco leaves in your bag for your ascent to the ancient ruins above your village.

You begin your journey, and as you climb up the mountain, you look over to the left and you see the terraced crops. You see the different things growing over there—and you see others from your village working very close to the Earth, working and tending the terraced gardens.

You continue onward and upward—rising into higher altitudes as you reach the top of the mountain. You climb through and eventually come up to an opening where you look around and see a beautiful building made out of stone. This building is open and spacious and it overlooks the vista of the Andes Mountains.

You walk into the open ruins and you can feel the sacred present within the atmosphere. As you walk around you see that there are sages, mediums, and elders saying their prayers, working their rituals and offering their sacred works to the great spirits and mysteries. The people here are in direct relationship with the otherworlds, and you can feel the presence of these other dimensions in this ancient site.

You pause and look out onto the vista of the valley below you, and as you take in this site, a priest and priestess come and welcome you as they both knew you were coming to undergo a vision quest. These elders welcome you and gift you with something—you reach out your hands and what do you receive? Perhaps it's a sacred stone, an herb, a feather, or a tool of power? Take a moment to discover your gift.

You give thanks for their gifts, and you reach inside your bag to bring out your own offering to them—thanking the priest and priestess for imparting their wisdom to you. The priest and priestess receive your gift and they guide you to a place within the ruins where you can undergo your vision quest.

You sit in this isolated area of the ruins and begin to breathe deeply.

As you breathe deeply, you feel the heat of the sun above you. It beams down warmth and life-force energy, and it shines brilliantly in the blue sky. Condors circle this brilliant light as if gathering and preparing the energies for you and your vision quest.

You hear the condors call above you, the villagers farming way down below, and you can smell the smoke of the elder's prayers burning in the ruin site. Just like the connection to the Earth and elements upon the start of your journey, you feel this connection to the spirits and beings around you—the condors, the farmers, the elders. All of life is within your field of consciousness. You breathe deeply and you know that you have merged the worlds of the Great Below with the Great Above within your heart space.

Your heart is the vessel for this unity consciousness and it is the sacred meeting place where two worlds become one. So as you drop into this field of consciousness, I invite you to offer your prayers to Inti—the sun god—and allow the energies of the Great Above to send you a message—a message for yourself, for your community, and for the world. Place your hand upon your heart and feel these messages, these direct transmissions from the Great Above, encode themselves within your heart and upon your DNA. You have received your vision from your quest.

You open your eyes and fully receive this download of your life. You find the priest and priestess and thank them for keeping the energies of this ancient temple alive so that these shamanic pathways can remain forever open. You offer your gratitude to these ancient wisdom keepers and you give thanks to the ancient temple itself, and you begin your return to the village.

You begin your descent, and you feel filled with sunlight, air, and clarity of vision, yet your feet are grounded firmly upon the Earth. You carefully make your way down to the village, walking past the river and nodding and smiling to those who are making their crafts. As you smile at them, you feel and remember your connection to the Earth around you and to the otherworlds above you. You feel these connections and know within your heart that you are a bridge between these worlds, and that the worlds of the Great Above and the Great Below merge together in your heart center. You acknowledge to yourself that you are a walker between these worlds and that you carry a strong medicine for the people—the medicine of this unity consciousness, love, and greater wisdom.

Take a deep breath, and exhale fully. Open your eyes and come back and feel your gratitude for this journey, for this experience, and for your connection to Pisac. Thank the mountain, river, village, and the sacred part of the southern region of the Sacred Valley.

Take a deep breath in and feel yourself return to your body. Grounded and centered within your physical body, open your eyes and fully return.

Take some time to journal, reflecting on your journey. Record your experiences.

▶▶◀◀

STAR WOLF SPEAKS

THE SEER'S CHAIR

When I first visited Pisac, I experienced a gestalt download. When my feet touched the lands of this high elevation, I instantly knew that the priests, seers, and astrologers resided within the mists of these tall mountains overlooking the village. As I walked the narrow path to the ruin, along the terraced gardens structured within the mountainside, I understood how the villagers and farmers living below grew the food for those living in the high mountains above. And, in one single moment of knowing, I understood that the farmers below knew how and when to plant the crops because of their relationship with the seers living above.

Once I had arrived at the ruins left behind by these ancient seers and astrologers, I remember being guided to the top of the mountain where there was a bench carved out of stone. This bench, and the ruin site of Pisac, are encapsulated by these colossal mountains, yet this specific site, especially the bench, is positioned in a way so that it overlooks the valley below and has a panoramic view of the sky above.

Our guide asked if I wanted to sit on this stone bench and connect to the energies of Pisac. I was the first of our group to sit on the bench, what I now call the "Seer's Chair." As I sat there with my eyes closed, I could feel a strong vibration going through my entire body. It started with my feet and then moved up through my legs, and all the way up the different vertebrae of my spine. Sitting in this Seer's Chair activated a kundalini awakening. My body was flooded with life-force energy, my third eye was activated, and I was catapulted into a visionary experience.

In my journey I could see a storyline playing out before my eyes. I was in Pisac in the times of ancient Peru. Walking through the different stone courtyards I could see how beautiful and full of life this village once was. And as I wandered around, I could sense a tragedy. I could sense that the conquerors had overtaken Pisac, both the agricultural village below and the astrological community above, and I knew that these people were taken from their homes and communities and enslaved.

Even sadder was the knowing that the ancient wisdom of these wise priests and seers had been pushed underground and kept hidden, as the conquerors did their best to eliminate the indigenous ways. This repression of the celestial knowledge had a ripple effect, and as time went on the farmers living in the village below—who were reliant upon the priests and seers living above—had to grow dependent upon the conquerors to grow the crops, as they had lost their connection with the stars and the heavens.

Historically we can look back and see a dramatic shift in agriculture after the conquerors invaded Pisac. Because these conquerors invaded this land, they disturbed the ways of the native people. They put a stop to their ceremonies and celebrations, they changed their crops, and they took away their spiritual traditions, practices, and wisdom. Being in Pisac and sitting in the Seer's Chair allowed me to see the deep sorrow and grief that is created when other cultures invade and dominate other cultures.

My experience in the Seer's Chair showed me how changing a culture's belief and lifestyle dramatically changed and wounded them. My journey and vision sitting in the Seer's Chair reminded me of humanity's ancestry, which is found within the stars. Pisac showed me how we are living in a time where we must remember our celestial origins—we must remember that we are star beings, and we must remember the wisdom that comes to us from the Great Above. It's time to once again allow our bodies, hearts, minds, and spirits to be planted with the wisdom of the heavens so that we may nurture and continue to grow these ancient mysteries here on Earth.

Pisac: A Sacred Homecoming
Ruby Falconer

Traveling to Peru is not without challenges, but I came prepared. Beforehand, I exercised, did a lot of walking, and listened to Vera when she suggested we purchase cans of oxygen at the Cuzco airport. As she said, "Why tough it out, when you don't have to?" A wise woman.

Vera Lopez, Linda Star Wolf, and Brad Collins were an amazing leadership team for our trip in December 2012. Our journey was chock-full of incredible experiences and powerful ceremonies at awe-inspiring sites. I was amazed—and I was not prepared for what happened at Pisac.

Just a little about me. I've been an astrologer since I was twenty-three and I've trained in many spiritual practices. For the last nineteen years I have been part of the Venus Rising staff and community. I am a Shamanic Breathwork master practitioner, and a shamanic minister and counselor. But I identify most with being an astrologer. I believe I've lived many lives as a practitioner of this art—and some of them I remember. When Vera told us that Pisac was where the Incan shaman priests had lived—the astrologer/astronomers—I was intrigued.

The ruins of Pisac are perched on the top of a mountain peak, about fifty miles from Machu Picchu and three and a half miles from the village of Pisac. Our bus brought us close, and we had to walk a fairly level incline the rest of the way. As we neared the archaeological ruins, I began to feel agitated—a sort of unexplained excitement. The elevation at Pisac is ten thousand feet; the air is thin. But the elevation did not account for this feeling; this was not oxygen deprivation. This was different.

We entered the site from a terrace that overlooked the rest of the ruins. Pisac is not a large area—from the upper level all of the existing ruins can be seen, spread along the rounded hill below. I'm a grounded person and while I've always been sensitive to the energies of vortexes and sacred sites, this feeling was unique—unlike anything I've experienced before or since. It was as though I could peer through the veils of time and "see" this place as it was a thousand years ago. I was so excited that I began running around—literally running; the effects of oxygen deprivation had completely vanished.

My friend Liz was watching me, amused and astonished. I told her what I was seeing—that the terrace above the village was where we'd sat in the evening, smoking our pipes. Our living quarters were behind the terrace. The open area beyond had been a ceremonial space. There had been columns ringing the area; I showed her where they were. The large curved stone now known as the "Seer's Chair" was an integral part of ceremony and ritual.

I ran through the lower levels—the structures open, their thatched roofs long gone. I knew the intended use of various rooms. Here was where we cleansed ourselves with water before going into ceremony. Here was where we used the smoke from a fire to cleanse and purge. This was a room for meditation. This was a storage room. And the great astronomical observatory in the center of the village—ah, this place—it hummed with an ancient vibration that I could feel when I put my hand on it. I spent many minutes with my ear pressed against it, listening to a deep rumble that emanated simultaneously from the core of the Earth and the unseen stars above.

All too soon, Rojo, my favorite guide, told us we had to go. I begged him for more time. I hadn't explored the whole site and I knew there was more. "Okay, yes," he said, "but only fifteen minutes." I raced to the end of the village, a promontory with a stunning view of the mountains beyond and the valley below. I knew I had stood at this spot many times before. By now I knew that I had experienced not just one lifetime in this magical place, but many. I had been a priest, an astrologer, an astronomer, a medicine man and woman, a mother, father, a leader, and a follower.

There had been a wall here that I had leaned against, lingering for hours, breathing in the spirits of the land. This was a place that I came to in order to be alone and to meditate. From this vantage point I could see supply caravans and messengers making their way up the mountain path. Pisac was isolated, and those teams delivering supplies and news were the source of great excitement in our village. I always knew when they were bringing information that was of importance to our community.

I knew that on one particular day I had stood in this place and watched as a single messenger ran barefoot up the steep mountain path. I knew he carried a message that would shatter my village and my life—but I could not remember what it was.

Later, back "home" in our beautiful resort in the valley, we did a Shamanic Breathwork session and I remembered. In the last of my many Peruvian lifetimes, I had been a young boy in Pisac. My father was the head shaman astronomer/astrologer. He was a trusted advisor to our king, and I was learning the shamanic ways from him. I was about ten years old, just at the beginning of my apprenticeship. I was with my father, standing at the far wall, when he saw the messenger running toward us. Something was wrong—I sensed it in the tension that immediately came into my father's body. This was a message he'd been expecting but hoped to never receive.

The invaders were coming. They had already cut a swath through our land and now they would come here. These were men who would not respect our ways and they were not far away. My father grabbed me and hurried home, back to our beautiful lodging with the terrace that looked out over the village and the mountains. "You must run," he told me. "Take some food and clothing. Run, and do not look back. Our ways must live through you."

I protested—I knew nothing. I had not yet been initiated into the deepest secrets of our tribe. "It will be enough," he told me. "It has to be. Now run."

I did as he said. I gathered up a bit of clothing and food and I ran. But I did not go far. I went to the outskirts of our rocky village and I stood and watched. The elders of our village were hiding things—sacred objects and medicine tools. But then suddenly the invaders were upon them and they showed no mercy. I did not see my father die, but I heard the screams and I saw the smoke. Our precious village was wrecked, our dwellings ransacked, the priests killed, and our women and children taken prisoner.

I turned and I ran.

I spent the rest of that life wandering, offering what I knew of our ancient rites to my people. I felt so inadequate; I knew so little. But the villages I visited knew who I was. They knew who my father was and where I came from. They welcomed me as a shaman priest of Pisac. They hid me from the angry eyes of the occupiers, who would have killed me if they could. I became invisible. The invaders did not see me. When our paths crossed, they saw only a ragged, dirty beggar, wandering across the countryside, living on scraps fed to him by those he encountered.

They did not know that in the dead of night, I shared the sacred rites I remembered and the rest I made up. I called upon my father and his fellow priests to speak through me. I do not know if anything I said or did was as it had been done when Pisac was beautiful and alive, but it was enough. That much I know. Through me, the spirit of our ancient mysteries stayed alive even if nothing else survived.

I never saw Pisac again, at least not in that lifetime. That day in December 2012 was a homecoming for the small Incan boy within me and the shaman astrologer priest he came to be. I will never forget.

MACHU PICCHU

University and Library of the Ancient Inca

ANCIENT, TIMELESS, AND OTHERWORLDLY—nothing is quite as shamanic as the ruin site of Machu Picchu. Discovered on July 24, 1911, by Hiram Bingham, an American archaeologist, Machu Picchu has captivated and magnetized many archaeologists, shamans, seekers, and tourists from around the world.

Suspended high up in the mountains above the Urubamba River, Machu Picchu is roughly fifty miles northwest of Cuzco at 8,040 feet (2,450 meters) altitude. Of all the temples and sacred sites established in the Andes, nothing holds as much mystery and wonder as Machu Picchu.

To date no one truly knows the true purpose and meaning of this ancient city and its various structures. Bingham suggests that Machu Picchu was built by an Incan king with the intention of serving the empire as a fortress. Other archaeologists suggest that Machu Picchu was built for Incan royalty, functioning much like a retreat center for the royals living in the Andes. When we look at these different theories and possibilities surrounding Machu Picchu, we must remember that these perspectives are all rooted in our modern-day viewpoint, which varies and differs from the perspectives shared by the ancients who built and resided within these stone walls.

What we do know about Machu Picchu is that at one time it was inhabited by the people of the Andes. Walking through these ruins we can see sections designated for agricultural and farming purposes, temples for religious ceremonies, and housing units to accommodate residential needs. Seeing that Machu Picchu was designed to accommodate these various facets of life we can know that at one time people lived in this city in the clouds.

We also know that Machu Picchu was abandoned. Based upon the remains and ruins found within this iconic ruin site, archaeologists are suggesting that those who lived in this city, high up in the mountains, all decided to leave Machu Picchu in one simultaneous moment. This mass exodus adds to the mystery of this lost Incan city. Not only do we lack the knowledge of this site's purpose and function in Incan society, we also do not understand why its inhabitants decided to completely abandon their home.

While these things remain a mystery to date, we can gather a lot of information from the things these people left behind. We can learn from their pottery, their stonework, and we can of course learn from their culture. When we look at Machu Picchu through the lens of the Andean cosmology and the principles and beliefs found in the Q'eros nation, we can begin to uncover and piece together some of Machu Picchu's mysteries.

MACHU PICCHU AS A UNIVERSITY

As with all sacred sites, temples, and cities in the Incan Empire, Machu Picchu was built with intention. When we look at its placement we can see that this construction was built in an ocean of mountains. Tucked in the mountains at such a high elevation, we can see how one of the intentions behind Machu Picchu was to connect with and channel the energy of the stars and the Star Nation. The Inca had a deep connection with the stars above. These ancient people identified as being the Children of the Sun, and they looked toward the heavens—the stars above—for guidance and direction. With this celestial connection, many people believe that Machu Picchu was a city whose primary purpose was to anchor heaven on earth—channeling the high energy and vibrations of the upper world and the stars onto our planet.

I believe that Machu Picchu was, and still is today, a university—a place where the ancients came to study advanced aspects of spirituality. Because this city was high up in the mountains, I believe that the residents living there were there to study the downloads and transmissions coming directly from the stars and cosmos—the Hanan Pacha. When the villagers, travelers, and established members of the Incan Empire came to Machu Picchu, they were coming to learn how to live in connection with the ancient arts of magic; they were learning how to live connected to heaven and earth. When people are living in an energetic field of high spirituality, they become like computers and begin downloading large amounts of cosmic wisdom and knowledge.

The Ñustas of Machu Picchu

Machu Picchu is a sanctuary that embodies the vibrations of the strong feminine. In archaeologist Marino Orlando Sánchez Macedo's book *De los sacerdotisas, brujas y adivinas de Machu Picchu* (The Priestesses, Witches and Psychics of Machu Picchu) he shares and suggests that the women living in Machu Picchu were not ordinary women; they were women who possessed strong psychic abilities and a deep knowledge of the natural world. Sánchez Macedo and others suggest that Machu Picchu was a temple where the high priestesses of the Incan Empire lived their lives. It was also a seat of learning for young women—the Ñustas—teaching them about the sacred ways of magic and mystery.

The Ñustas of Machu Picchu were young girls who came to Machu Picchu from all over the Incan Empire to study the ancient arts of magic. These young girls were chosen by their villages and communities because they demonstrated an innate connection to the land as well as heightened psychic abilities. By journeying to Machu Picchu, these young women would study from the high priestesses of Machu Picchu and learn how to live life with intention and in a sacred manner.

The high priestesses of Machu Picchu trained the Ñustas to become priestesses and medicine women so that they could go back to their villages and offer spiritual guidance and services to their community. The high priestesses showed these young women how to cook meals, weave fabrics, and prepare the altar so that they might live in alignment with the sacred ways of the Inca. The Ñustas learned how to live life in a high spiritual vibration.

In addition to learning how to live life in a sacred manner, the Ñustas were also trained how to work with the frequencies and energies of the Earth and the heavens above. The Ñustas learned about the ceke lines coursing through the Earth, and the priestesses taught them how they could alter these energies by placing different rocks and stones on specific points of power. The Ñustas also learned how to align to the energies of the cosmos and use the heavens above as a tool for guidance and direction.

It was believed that by just living in Machu Picchu, these young women experienced an expansion and growth of their psychic and spiritual abilities. So it was a great honor to be chosen by their village to journey to Machu Picchu and further their studies of the ancient arts so that they could become the wise women and priestesses of their communities.

THE ANCIENT HIDDEN LIBRARY AND GUARDIANS OF LIGHT

Archaeologists have discovered systems of tunnels underneath the surface of both Machu Picchu and Huayna Picchu. When I first journeyed to Peru, Chuma—the high priestess of Machu Picchu who was channeled by Luiz Gasparetto—spoke about an ancient hidden library there. She shared that this library contains the knowledge, wisdom, and science of the past, the present, and the future. In my journeys to Machu Picchu, both astral journeys and physical journeys, I have come to know and believe that Machu Picchu holds a hidden library of knowledge underneath its surface and this ancient wisdom is guarded by a tribe of the light beings living beneath these ruins.

As I have walked through the relics of Machu Picchu, I have been able to connect with the spirits of this site. On my own, through meditation or journey work, I have discovered a tribe of guardians living in the tunnels underneath the city. I first connected with these beings more than thirty years ago. I was walking through Machu Picchu by myself, and I found a quiet place in the ruin site to meditate and journey. In my journey, I was taken to the tunnel systems below the city. Throughout these tunnels I could see large quantities of emerald, amethyst, and clear quartz crystals. Moving throughout these tunnels were these high-frequency beings; they were moving so fast and vibrating so high that at first I was only able to see them out of the corner of my eye. Over my years of working with the energies of Peru, especially Machu Picchu, I have come to understand that these beings are a high frequency—they are vibrating outside of my physical time, space, and dimension.

These guardians are unlike any being I have ever seen. They are rather short beings ranging anywhere between three to four feet in height, and their shape is without form—they are more of a vibration than a physical structure. As I have developed a relationship with them, they have shared with me that their purpose is to guard and protect the hidden wisdom living at Machu Picchu; specifically, guarding and protecting its ancient library.

These beings have shared with me that the wisdom and knowledge living in this library contains the science of the past, present, and future. They have shared with me that this knowledge and information is what humanity is searching for; it's the knowledge of our full human potential. I have asked these beings why this information has been kept hidden all these years. In reply, they told me that humanity is still not ready to receive the wisdom and knowledge about who they really are. These beings believe that humanity's current state of consciousness would misuse the information about our full potential, or we would simply just not believe it.

I believe that this ancient library, and its wisdom, is still hidden in Machu Picchu. I believe that it has not yet been discovered because, as these beings have shared with me, humanity is still not ready for higher levels of wisdom. In the past, our ancient ancestors formulated a strong connection with nature, the stars, and the divine. They built their monolithic temples without our modern-day technology, and these ancient structures are still standing. Our ancestors contributed to our future by storing this wisdom for us to discover and glean from.

Examining the lives of our ancestors and recognizing the vastness of their simple yet deeply profound contributions to our existence leaves me contemplating what we (modern-day) people are leaving behind. What legacies, what stories, what advances are we contributing to the collective growth and development of our species?

The wisdom of Machu Picchu—both that which is accessible and the hidden knowledge in this ancient library—has the ability to shift and accelerate the consciousness on our planet.

THE MAGIC, ALCHEMY, AND EXPERIENCES OF MACHU PICCHU

Machu Picchu has an alchemy to it. Being in the energetic field of Machu Picchu allows us to raise our vibration and experience our own connection to divine wisdom. The experience of Machu Picchu awakens something in us; I believe it awakens our full potential as human beings and aligns us with the vibration of our ancient shamanic ancestors.

Machu Picchu Has Her Own Plan for You
Madeleine Marentette

People travel to Machu Picchu for many different reasons. When you are called to Machu Picchu you will indeed get a sense that you are going on a once-in-a-lifetime quest to enrich your mind, heart, and spirit. You also get a sense that something special is waiting for you, but that you shouldn't even bother to try and guess what that might be beforehand.

In 2008 I partnered with Vera Lopez to organize and lead sacred journeys for women. Thirty-three women joined us in what would be our first journey to Peru. Vera has a special way of introducing her groups to the breathtaking vistas and the presence that is Machu Picchu. She kept her surprise from the group and from me as well, and I am grateful for it.

When I was finally introduced to Machu Picchu, my knees buckled and I sank instantly to the ground. Sobbing. This doesn't happen to me. But I allowed it, and knew I had to. I sobbed until I could sob no more.

As I gathered my thoughts and wiped the blur from my eyes I looked out upon the vista, acknowledging the deep purge and the feelings of uncontainable spiritual reverence. My tears were for Mother Earth. For the first time in my life I connected with the mother as one, in true spiritual form. I had pierced the veil between heaven and earth. She and I were united. I was she and she was me. I witnessed and felt the inhale and exhale of her breath. I witnessed and felt her etheric light. I witnessed and felt her grand, overseeing presence and her work to sustain humanity. In that moment I had unlocked a treasure that I didn't realize I was seeking or required for my future work in continued service.

My dedication as an activist for people, animals, and the planet deepened as a result of this journey to the mother. As I said, when you hear her call you, you will feel compelled to go. But you will waste your time trying to find the answer as to why she is calling you. Until you arrive.

⤙⤚

STAR WOLF SPEAKS

12-12-12 MACHU PICCHU EXPERIENCE

In 2012, Vera and I along with my beloved late husband Brad Collins orchestrated a shamanic journey to Peru. We set the dates so that we could take our group of soul friends and family to Machu Picchu on 12-12-12 and witness the sunrise. We knew that this date, 12-12-12, was an auspicious one that announced the opening of a multidimensional portal. From a numerological perspective the date 12-12-2012 reduces down to the number 56, which is reduced down even further to the master number 11. The number 11 is believed to carry the frequency of greater insight, access to esoteric information, and empathy. Symbolically, 11 is understood to represent a portal, or a doorway where higher energies from other dimensions can enter.

With all of this symbolism and synchronicity around our trip dates, Vera and I were able to magnetize a large size group for this shamanic journey to Peru. Many people from all over the world felt called to this specific journey, and in the end, our group represented fifteen different countries. Together as a tribe of worldly ambassadors we would be journeying to Machu Picchu to open the portals of 12-12-12 and anchor the energies coming through this portal so that they could support and accelerate Earth's planetary transformation.

On the early morning of 12-12-12, our group gathered in Aguas Calientes—the village at the foothills of Machu Picchu. We all planned to wear white in honor of our journey and mission to anchor more light on Earth. As a group we boarded our bus and began our ascent to the lost city of the Inca. Our group was on a sacred pilgrimage. Collectively, we had a date with destiny, and our souls had contracted with one another to be a part of this sacred mission. Our intention and the heart of our mission was to support the opening of the 12-12-12 portal so that we could all infuse the Earth with as much energy as possible—supporting Pachamama in her own rebirth process.

We snaked our way up through the mountains in the predawn darkness and fog, arriving at Machu Picchu before sunrise. When we got there, we were surprised to be greeted by the Q'eros shamans who had been traveling with us. As we were planning our sunrise pilgrimage to Machu Picchu, they had not been able to join us, but Great Mystery created magic and our paqos—the Q'eros shamans—were able to join us for this special sunrise journey.

Our group journeyed in the dark and through the fog. With each member dressed in white, we silently made our way through the ancient ruins of Machu Picchu and arrived at the site known as the "shaman's hut." This site is usually off-limits to the general public but because we were onsite in the early morning hours, we were able to enter this ancient place of power.

The shaman's hut has a thatched roof top and an earthen floor. The walls have a few windows that overlook the mountains surrounding Machu Picchu. Together we entered this hut and arranged ourselves in a circle, still held within the predawn darkness. Remaining in reverence and silence, we stared off into the misty mountains and began to go into deep ceremony.

There was this palpable feeling of electricity coursing through the air as the shamans began to smudge us. Anticipation and excitement buzzed within us, yet there was simultaneously an unspoken desire for silence and the space necessary to be internal. As the morning unfolded, we began to sing. The shamans sang their Quechua songs, and different people in our group shared special songs from their different countries. Brad, my late husband, began to play his flute, which matched a Peruvian tone, and we were all catapulted into the mystery of this experience.

The shamans began to say their prayers, inspiring each of us to offer prayers in our own tongue and language. The shamans used their holy water and went around our group offering blessings. At different times people felt moved to touch one another's heart space—amplifying the field of love and mystery. At times there were different tones, moans, groans, and wolf howls released from different members of our group—nothing about this ceremony had been planned beforehand. From the moment we entered the shaman's hut and formed our sacred circle, we collectively dove into an open ceremony that was orchestrated and guided only by divine province. Everything about this open ceremony flowed. Nothing was structured and no one person was facilitating the ceremony—we came together as a tribe and we each offered and shared our medicine, our songs, our prayers, and our blessings with one another.

As the sun rose up over the mountains and light began to enter through the windows of the shaman's hut, everyone in our group began to sing the Beatles song "Here Comes the Sun." This moment was truly epic as we witnessed the sun rise up over Machu Picchu, and witnessed the opening of the 12-12-12 portal. On this journey, Vera had gifted me with a special wand for my birthday. It's decorated with the symbols found in the Egyptian cosmology, a pantheon I am deeply connected to. Vera's wand possesses the symbols found in the Andean cosmology. Together, with our wands, we toasted each other and opened the portals of 12-12-12 for the transformation of our planet—I was one pillar of this portal and Vera was another.

At one point, Brad entered the center of the circle and he continued playing his flute and began to dance around. In this moment he looked like the Greek god Dionysus. There was a light around him, which was seen by several people of the group. Brad shared with me later that this moment was one of the most joyous moments in his life, and he felt as if he were completely fulfilling his destiny—playing his flute on top of

Machu Picchu, with the Q'eros shamans in the shaman's hut on 12-12-12, dancing as the sun rose up over the mountains.

In some ways we thought we had only been in the shaman's hut for an hour and a half, but once we had finished our ceremony and began our descent back down to the village below, we realized that we had been in the hut with the shamans for over four hours. For four hours, we were all deeply entranced in our sunrise ceremony. No one in our group asked to go to the bathroom and no one in our group needed to leave, felt fatigued, or even needed to eat. We were all encapsulated in the high vibrational energy of this epic moment in time and history—a powerful (and altering) sunrise ceremony at Machu Picchu on 12-12-12. This memory will always be in my heart, and I know each member of our worldly group is cherishing it within their hearts as well.

Throughout my thirty years of facilitating spiritual journeys to Peru, I have had the opportunity to witness people from different countries, cultures, and walks of life experience a profound shift in consciousness upon visiting Machu Picchu. People from all over the world journey to Machu Picchu and they experience the feeling of a spiritual presence surround them. Walking through these ruins, they feel as if they can speak in tongues or in different, other-worldly languages that they've never heard before. They remember past-life experiences, and they have a deep knowing that something has called their souls back to this sacred land. What I know and believe to be true is that Machu Picchu calls those who are ready, and when those of us answer the call, Machu Picchu activates the seeds of light living within one's luminous field. It doesn't matter who you are, where you come from, or what age you are—Machu Picchu activates and shifts your consciousness.

THE MOST PRECIOUS GIFT
FROM MACHU PICCHU

Peru is a sacred land that holds medicine for the heart. The medicine of Peru provides us with lessons and experiences that open the heart and deepen the spirit. These lessons and experiences often disguise themselves within simple moments and humble exchanges; manifesting as a butterfly, a stone, a hummingbird, and the smile of a young child.

It was my third journey to Peru when I experienced the potency of Peru's heart medicine. Even though it was my third time, I still looked forward to this journey as if it were my first. Even today when I journey to Peru and share these ancient mysteries with others, the spirit of the Andes Mountains and this sacred land is always "new" to my eyes and heart.

My third journey to Peru happened in February 1990. It was the rainy season in Peru. Even though February is considered summertime in South America, Peru really only has two seasons—the dry season and the wet season. And when it rains in Peru, it rains. But the rain did not squander the excitement within our group!

At the time, Peru, and Machu Picchu specifically, had not yet reached the awareness of the mass consciousness. But even though there were fewer tourists and travelers visiting than there are today, our group still had to wait in line for a bus to take us up the mountain.

As we stood waiting for a bus to arrive, I felt as if I were being watched. I casually looked around, and I locked with the most soul-piercing eyes I have ever seen. Sitting right there in front of me on an old cold stone bench was a little girl about seven years old. She was a pretty girl with a vivacious smile and bright, beautiful eyes. This young girl was watching the tourists walk by and wait in line to catch the next bus. Our eyes connected a couple of times, as there was so much energy coming from her that I could not stop myself from finding her gaze. I, a thirty-two-year-old woman at the time, was captured by this young girl's presence. There was something so mysterious yet strangely familiar about this young girl, but I couldn't put my finger on it.

The line was not moving, there was nothing to do but wait, and our eyes met once again. This time the girl spoke to me.

"What is your name?" she asked me with a brilliant smile and no hesitation.

"I am Vera. What is your name?" I replied.

"My name is Imasumac. It means 'the prettiest one,'" she shared.

She definitely lived up to the meaning of her name—she was so pretty and I was fascinated by her as she continued to speak, placing me under her spell.

I was not the only one captivated by Imasumac's presence; my entire group was magnetized by her. Imasumac asked for each of our names, and she welcomed us to Machu Picchu—"the most important Incan temple of all times," she shared with us. Imasumac continued to talk to us as we waited in line for the next bus. She talked and talked, speaking quickly with so much to say. We listened to her, enamored by her beauty and cuteness.

The next bus came and we all felt disappointed that we had to part ways with Imasumac. As we rode up the mountain our group could not stop talking about her. She truly was a special child, like none I have ever encountered before. Our bus arrived at Machu Picchu and our group experienced the initial magic of this sacred site.

When I take groups to Peru I intentionally dedicate at least three days for us to explore Machu Picchu, one of the world's seven wonders. This allows journeyers the opportunity to fully connect with this place of power. Through the years I've learned that while each of Peru's sacred sites and temples has the ability to shift and alter our lives, none of them can compete with the power held within the sacredness of Machu Picchu.

As we explored Machu Picchu, I could not stop thinking of Imasumac. She was such an intense child and her beauty was undeniable. Her sweet voice, smile, and her vibrant presence stayed with me as I walked throughout the ruins.

When we left Machu Picchu for the day, as I exited the gate, I heard a sweet voice like a hummingbird humming my name. And there was Imasumac, standing outside the entrance to Machu Picchu, waiting for me.

I could not believe my eyes—what was she doing in the parking lot outside Machu Picchu? When she saw me, she ran to me and embraced me with a hug.

"I missed you so much," Imasumac said to me. "I knew I was going to see you again."

I held her in my arms, and as we hugged I felt this deep connection emerge from within me. I have never felt a connection like this before.

"I missed you, too," I told her. "What are you doing here?"

Imasumac told me that she was there for a birthday celebration; the father of one of the village girls worked at the hotel located just outside of Machu Picchu's entrance, and he was giving his daughter a special birthday party.

We parted ways again as our bus arrived to take us down to the bottom of the mountain, and Imasumac found her way to her friend's birthday celebration. Again, as we parted, I felt this deep longing within me wishing that we could connect longer with one another. She stayed within my heart and my mind's eye, and I wondered if our paths would cross again.

Back then, to travel from Machu Picchu station to the village of Aguas Calientes we had to walk about thirty minutes along the old train tracks. This walk was actually a lot of fun, and to me it always felt like a walking meditation. When we arrived at the small village we decided to stop at the plaza and eat something before getting to our lodge. Soon after, the night had come and it was time to sleep. Our lodge was just a few blocks away from the restaurant, and upon our arrival we were once again surprised by a visit from Imasumac. This time she was accompanied by her mother, Margpht. Our group smiled at the site of Imasumac and we all flocked to her and her mother. Imasumac rushed toward me and gave me a hug. I couldn't help but stare at her; she looked like a little Incan princess.

She introduced us all to Margpht, who was a sweet and humble woman. I felt a connection with Imasumac's mother right away. Margpht apologized for bothering us, and she shared that Imasumac would not leave her alone until she met me and our group.

After the two previous and short encounters, we all understood that we were in the presence of a one-of-a-kind child of the Andes—and that she could always get what she wanted. Imasumac felt comfortable and at home with me and our group. She began sharing stories with us and telling us all about the mysteries of Machu Picchu, the holy mountains of the Andes, the sacred herbs and magical healing plants

118 ◄ The Sacred Land and Temples of Peru

found throughout the land, and the importance of women within the ancient Incan culture. Even though we were tired after a long day traveling from Cuzco to Machu Picchu, spending the day in the sacred site, and experiencing all the profound emotions we did, we did not dare to stop or interrupt her. We were all captured by the magic and knowledge coming from this little girl.

"How does she know all of this?" I asked her mother.

"I have no idea. We've never taught her about any of this. She's talked about all of this stuff since she could talk." Imasumac's mother informed us. "She actually goes around teaching everyone about this information. She's the little medicine woman of our village."

Imasumac's mother continued to tell us that Imasumac was notorious for disappearing for short lengths of time only to come back to the village with medicinal herbs and plants for different people within their village. Imasumac just knew what each person needed to make them healthy and well; no one would tell her that they were sick or not feeling well, yet she knew exactly what they needed.

"Everyone in our village knows that Imasumac is no ordinary child," her mother told us.

We continued to listen to Imasumac, absorbing all of her wisdom and information. One topic would lead into another, and she would navigate through each discussion sharing information with us that takes many people lifetimes to learn and acquire. We all sat there within the lobby of our lodge captivated by the presence of this wise little being.

Imasumac looked over to me and touched my hair, "I want my hair to grow just like yours. It reminds me of when we lived here before—your hair and mine were both so long." I looked at her with deep awe, and I knew what she meant. Our souls knew each other in a past life, and here we were connected with each other once again.

The next two days our group went back to Machu Picchu. During these two days my heart was so divided between my group, my own experiences, and Imasumac's intense presence. When it came time for our group to leave Machu Picchu and Aguas Calientes, I found it so difficult to say goodbye to Imasumac. Just a few days before, my life had felt simple and uncomplicated, but after connecting with this little being I knew I would never be able to live exactly the same. My heart was different because of Imasumac; I felt as if she were a part of me and vice versa.

I found her home within the village. Her mother was so honored to have me there and when I went to hug Imasumac and say my farewells I started crying. Imasumac hugged me, and I felt as if her entire body and presence entered my heart.

"You know there is no distance between us, and we can meet any-time we want to, right?" I heard her sweet wisdom whisper in my ear.

"Yes, of course we can," I whispered back to her, totally knowing what she meant.

We said our farewells and parted ways. I learned later that she cried for hours after I left, and she didn't stop talking about me. For years when I arrived in Aguas Calientes the first thing I did was rush up the only street in the village screaming her name. The natives helped spread the word that I was back, and Imasumac and I would always find each other whenever I returned.

After the first year when I returned to Machu Picchu, Imasumac's mother told me that she would love to give me Imasumac as my god-daughter, but she could not do so because of a promise she made long before.

Within Peru, as in most of South America, the baptism of a child is a serious act. To baptize a child is to assume a certain level of respon-sibility for that child; should anything happen to the child's parents, his or her godparents (the ones who baptized the child) assume respon-sibility for the care of the child. The godparents are also expected to provide spiritual support and a safe place to come when the child is in need of advice. To be invited as a godparent is holy and something very special; no one takes this invitation for granted. Throughout my thirty-one years of travels to Peru, I have been asked to baptize hundreds of children. The locals make it a point to have foreigners baptize their children with hopes that their children will be well taken care of should anything happen to them. Throughout these years, I have baptized only two children: Hampi, Imasumac's daughter; and John Salas, the son of my dear friend and respected shaman Don Wilbert.

Margpht shared with me that even though she and her husband would be honored to have me as part of their family and as Imasumac's godmother, she couldn't give Imasumac to me because she was already taken, they had offered her to the rainbow. I learned that when Imasumac was born it was raining in Machu Picchu, and soon after her birth the clouds opened up to show a rainbow in the sky. Imasumac's mother took her and held Imasumac to the sky, asking Grandfather Rainbow to take Imasumac in his light and bless her life's path.

Imasumac's mother told me, "So we can't give her to you in baptism, but I know that even though I gave birth to her, she is your daughter and you are her mother—her soul mother, her spiritual mother."

These words touched and humbled my heart. Here was the person who gave birth to this special soul, and she was acknowledging the timeless connection shared between me and Imasumac. I knew she was right; while I did not give birth to this precious being, I knew within my heart that she was indeed my spiritual daughter.

Imasumac accompanied me through many of my visits to the sanctuary of Machu Picchu. She was always ready to join us and guide us through all of the special places hidden within the city. During one of the first meditations I led in Machu Picchu that she was invited to join, she acted like she knew what to do. She followed the instructions with ease—closing her eyes and breathing deeply, and she allowed Spirit to show her a message. After the meditation we went around our group and shared our different experiences. When it was time for Imasumac to share her experience, she said that she had a visionary memory where I was an elder and she was a little girl. She shared that she and I were holding hands and coming down the mountain a long, long time ago. She spoke of this past-life vision of hers with such simplicity and grace; this state of connection and consciousness was seemingly natural to her.

Throughout my many years of journeying to Peru, I have been blessed with hundreds of spiritual gifts and I have received thousands of blessings. This sweet Andean princess and the connection we share is definitely the most precious treasure that I've received from Machu Picchu.

SHAMANIC JOURNEY
TO MACHU PICCHU
Guided by Vera Lopez

Take a deep breath and close your eyes. Exhale fully and allow yourself to become fully present—right here and right now. We are going on a journey, a sacred journey to the heart of Machu Picchu. Open your mind's eye and imagine traveling to this sacred land and to this sacred place. Breathing in and breathing out, you can see in your mind's eye that it is still early morning. It is dark, yet we know that today is the day we've been waiting for. Today is the day we return to the heart of the mother; we return to the ancient university of Machu Picchu.

We are at the door of the ancient city of light. We are wearing white and we feel ready to take this journey. In our hearts there is pure peace, serenity, trust, and deep joy; we feel the honor of returning. The principal gate opens for us and we walk along the path before us, knowing this journey well from lifetimes before. We walk gently, and even though it is still very early and dark, the morning sun has not yet broken through the mountains, and we can still see everything.

As we walk, we follow the high path to where we can deeply connect to the entire city, and we open our hearts to the majesty that is Machu Picchu.

And as we walk this path, we smell the beautiful rainforest. It is a perfume so characteristic of Machu Picchu. The Earth smells fresh. The vegetation smells alive, and we feel the presence of Great Mystery. We feel the presence of the ancient ones. All the living beings that have shared the sacred university with us in the past are walking this path with us. We can feel their spirits rejoicing with our homecoming.

We are connected to the invisible worlds, and the spirits of Machu Picchu; they are journeying alongside us. We feel and we see their presence. We even hear their giggling of joy, of happiness—celebrating with us this sacred initiation.

We take a deep breath, and look around, realizing that time has passed so quickly and we are now on the highest point of Machu Picchu. We close our eyes for a moment. We feel the ground below us, and we feel the roots that we have in this place. It is an ancient home for our souls. We feel the connections we have with this sacred mountain. There is a love here that we have never felt anywhere before. It is a love that nurtures us and speaks directly to our hearts. We feel grounded and centered.

We stand tall and we feel the vibration outside of us as we continue with our eyes closed. We feel the vibration outside of us organizing the magic to welcome us back. So as we stand at this point, at the highest place of Machu Picchu, we go deeper and deeper into the inner silence and expand all the senses of our being. We feel our pineal gland opening up the gifts of our intuition—the gifts of our knowing, the gifts that remind us of all the thousands and thousands of years that we have spent in the expansion of our consciousness.

We become so present. We feel our physical body, our light body, so alive, and we expand both the vibration of the physical and the vibration of the light body, like a big egg of light all around us from below, entering the grounds of Machu Picchu and from above going all the way to Hanan Pacha. We are in the big egg of life. We open our arms, and we hear the "Yes" to open our eyes and see the sun rising above the beautiful, sacred mountains.

We see the sun breaking through and shining upon Machu Picchu's ancient stones. We see the light touch the stones and turn everything to gold. The stones are shining and glistening in the light. The grass is greener and the illumination is so high that we know that we are in the seat of crystals, the seat of life. We are in the city of the clouds. The mist is opening magically in front of our eyes. We hear the birds of Machu Picchu singing songs of welcome. We feel the presence of Chuma, the high priestess of this sacred site, as well as the elder council, the shamans, priestesses, and Ñustas. These wise and ancient beings are here to welcome us into the shamanic mysteries of Machu Picchu. We are in this great awe as we are once again remembering all the initiations that we have received here before. These memories and these powerful beings support us in forgiving ourselves for forgetting who we really are; they are here to support us in taking back ownership of our divine self.

Each chakra in our physical body is open as a vortex spinning with light, receiving and downloading ancient wisdom that is vibrating every-where in Machu Picchu. We are not only receiving the physical energies of Machu Picchu, we are also tapping into the energies of the astral realms—the etheric dimensions of this crystal city of light. For there is a Machu Picchu that we see, and there is a Machu Picchu that we feel. We are interconnected with both of these energies, and there is an exchange of sacredness going on—in and out between us and this city in the clouds.

As we welcome this day, we feel the warmth of the sun on our skin. We feel the light of the sun touching our heart, and we feel the guid-ance from the holy women of Machu Picchu as well as the presence of the great grandmothers and Apus guiding us to come down these sacred steps, going all the way through the sacred plaza. We move very fast down these steps. Like light beings, we move in front of the Temple of the Condor.

We stand in front of the presence of Condor—the presence of Hanan Pacha. Under the wings of Condor, we are guided to crawl through a small entrance. This entrance is the portal to the Ukhu Pacha of Machu Picchu. As we enter this portal, we hear voices of the light beings that live within the ancient tunnels, and we are being granted permission to walk through this portal.

So we walk through it and we know that there are many rooms and today we are going to go through a special room. We allow a light being to guide us to where the gift of today lies. And we trust this being because we know this being from many lives and many, many years ago—years that are cosmic. Light years. It is a return into the past, the present, and the future, and here we find a room. The room is made of ancient walls of stone but they are really light and transparent. This is the mystery of the ancient library. It is made of light, and it reminds us of what we are made of. In the center of this room we find a white table made of a special stone.

We approach the stone, and we put our hands onto it, and as we do we start to feel a transmission of ancient wisdom into us. For a moment we feel ourselves traveling into this zone of no time and no space, and we remember very clearly this beginning of everything. The transmission of this ancient library is helping us to remember who we truly are by remembering that in the beginning we were the light. We came from a point of light and we traveled through entirety to choose the point of individuality where we separated from one light into many particles of light to experience a new perspective on Creation.

The ancient wisdom of this library is showing us the secrets of the past, the present, and the future. In this, we are meant to totally be a part of what is right here and right now, because everything is happening all at once. The deeper we remember who we are, the more we are willing to dive deeper into the light within. The more we are able to connect with our whole, inner wisdom, the more we are able to access the entire wisdom of the universe. Because we are it. We are the knowledge. We are the library, we are the light, and here are the stones in our hands. We become one with this room and this frequency, and this is the gift of this library. It unifies our fields with everything. In this, we have an awareness that the separation happens as a choice and the unification also happens as a choice. We can come back to the oneness and we can come into the individuality as we choose.

At this moment it is all clear to us—we know that when we go to the field of oneness everything is available to us, and we can choose to bring the energetic field of oneness back into our individual expression and manifestation; there is no need for fragmentation. Within this space, we also know that the great wisdom within the field of oneness is always available to us, even when it seems absent; we know that this absence is just an illusion. This ancient library reminds us that all of this wisdom is always available within us, and when we trust this knowing, we will obtain the wisdom we need for our divine purpose. We feel in this moment the self-empowerment of being connected to our true selves. And in this deep silence of the void, of the beginning of everything and the eternal of all, we return to the point of light inside of our hearts. We return to our body, knowing that we know the secret that Machu Picchu holds is the secret of remembering who it is we truly are: both universe and human, and god and goddess of Creation.

The secret libraries of Machu Picchu are the portals we need to return to the all as a choice and to be in the individuality as a choice, knowing that in the one or in the individuality, the wisdom of everything is always available to us. We can access this wisdom through our intention. In this moment we choose to continue to journey as individuals and we give reverence to the beings of light that are with us in this room and allowing us to go through this remembering. In this blessed moment we find ourselves guided back to the hallway that takes us out of the portal outside the Temple of the Condor. We know, with great joy, that Machu Picchu is always vibrating into this high frequency and we can access its heart and its secret of oneness and individuality at any time.

We can journey through this portal as a reminder of how to access and journey into this integration. We return into the seed of who we are right now. And we travel deep and fast into our physical body that is in the center of Machu Picchu. Breathing in and out, back into our body wherever we are sitting right now. And feeling the awareness of this journey and the joy and the magic of knowing that we truly experience the sunrise in Machu Picchu and the activation of the sacred library and our activation of the crystal in the center of Machu Picchu. With this, we have the intention to remember that all beings here are one. We bring all of this together into right here and right now. And we trust that we are the avatars, that we are the shamans, that we are the healers, that we are the enlightened beings. We have the medicine, the power, and the gift to really remember who we are and facilitate others to do the same. And together, declare heaven on earth—and so it is.

THE ICA REGION

Dr. Cabrera and the Ica Stones

ON THE COASTLINE OF LIMA is the Ica region of Peru. In this region there are five provinces (or regions of land), the largest of which is the province of Ica. In the late 1960s, Doctor Javier Cabrera lived at Ica. Throughout my many journeys to Peru, I was fortunate to have formed a direct relationship with Dr. Cabrera. On some of my journeys, I would take my groups to his museum of Ica stones and receive Cabrera's direct download about these ancient, yet highly advanced engraved stones. Throughout my years of friendship with Cabrera, I was able to receive his direct transmission of knowledge, experience, and history of working with the Ica stones. In our friendship he shared with me the story of how he was led to these ancient stones, and how these stones shifted his pacha—his life's journey—from that of being a highly acclaimed medical doctor to working with these ancient stones. They have proved that our physical world is much older than modern science attests.

To honor his pacha (his life) and to continue his legacy I am sharing Cabrera's story below.

Born in 1924, Dr. Cabrera was the child of a wealthy and successful family. He studied medicine and became a medical doctor, establishing a practice in the Ica province of Peru. In his medical practice, he offered various charity check-ups and treatments to local citizens who were unable to afford his medical services. Because ayni is an ingrained principle and value in the culture of Peru, the local people would offer

Cabrera exchanges and trades, gifting him with chickens, eggs, avocados, or something else that was of value to them, so that they could be in right relationship and in ayni with Dr. Cabrera.

Over the course of time, in his practice Cabrera received an unusual stone with a highly advanced carving on it. He received this stone from a man in exchange for attending to the medical needs of this man's wife. Cabrera's fascination for this stone grew the more he examined the engravings, and he knew that this stone was not something available in the local market.

Cabrera asked the man about its origins. The man shared that he acquired the stone in the local market. Challenging the man's answer, Cabrera asked again about the origins of the stone.

The man grew silent and then told Dr. Cabrera that before he disclosed this information he needed to secure the requisite permission to do so.

Dr. Cabrera obliged and waited for him to return after obtaining permission.

A couple days went by before the man returned to Dr. Cabrera's office. He informed Dr. Cabrera that he had permission to disclose the origins of the stone, but rather than telling him about the stone's origins, the man said he would take Dr. Cabrera to the site where he'd found the engraved stone.

The man had Dr. Cabrera promise him that he would never disclose the origins and location of these stones. Dr. Cabrera knew he had to give his personal word and honor his oath of secrecy in order for this humble man to trust him with the location and origin of these mysterious stones.

Dr. Cabrera complied with the man's request, and they began their journey.

Dr. Cabrera and the man made their way to a cave. Inside this cave Dr. Cabrera found hundreds and thousands of stones engraved in the same style as the one he had received from the man. In this cave, Dr. Cabrera found stones of different shapes and sizes, yet all had deeply intricate designs engraved upon them. Each stone depicted a different scene and image. As Dr. Cabrera would shortly discover, each of these stones held cosmic wisdom and the pictographs carved on them documented the history of the planet and of humanity.

After being in the cave for a while and absorbing all of the images found upon the stones, Dr. Cabrera remembered that the man had to request permission from someone, or something, to bring him here.

Cabrera asked the man, "Whose permission did you have to obtain in order to bring me here?"

"Do you really want to know?" the man asked.

"Yes," Dr. Cabrera replied.

The man looked around the cave, and then said, "It's all right. You can come out now."

A couple of moments after the man made this announcement, the cave began to fill itself with light beings. Coming out of crevices and from behind rocks these light beings surrounded the man and Dr. Cabrera.

I remember Dr. Cabrera's face when he was telling me this story. "Can you imagine the look on my face when I saw those light beings for the first time?" he asked me. "Me, a doctor and disbeliever in this kind of local superstition? To this day I still chuckle when I remember my own reaction."

Dr. Cabrera continued his story by saying, "These beings started to talk to me using telepathy, which was another new experience I knew nothing about. As these beings continued to communicate with me, telepathy began to feel normal and familiar to me. The light beings confirmed that the engraved stones in the cave were made by ancient and advanced civilizations, and that the images on the stones detailed the history of the world and of humanity." The light beings told Dr. Cabrera that they had been waiting for him to arrive and disclosed to him that he was destined to bring forth, to the larger public, the cosmic wisdom found on these stones.

After his experience in the cave with the stones and the light beings, Dr. Cabrera returned to his home in Ica and established a museum to house the stones. His entire life changed as he became devoted to serving this sacred purpose given to him by the light beings and the stones. When he shared this information with the public, some people thought he was crazy. To this day, some people still do, and they look for ways to discredit him. Others, like Erich Von Däniken—the bestselling author of *Chariots of the Gods*—saw his brilliance. Von Däniken interviewed Cabrera and brought more awareness to the Ica Stones and to Dr. Cabrera's body of work. All of the dynamics that come with both of these polarities (positive and negative) entered his life—his wife left him, his son committed suicide, and Dr. Cabrera faced each obstacle with dignity. He knew that he had made a promise to a purpose much larger than himself, and regardless of what other people thought of him, he was dedicated to sharing his sacred work with others, welcoming all those open to learning to his museum. Dr. Cabrera maintained his commitment to his sacred purpose until he died in December of 2001. Today his daughter continues his legacy by maintaining the museum of Ica Stones that he created.

During his time on Earth, Dr. Cabrera never disclosed the location of the cave that had held the stones or the light beings. There are many articles about Dr. Cabrera and the Ica Stones, and some of these writings suggest that Cabrera's discovery and work with these stones is fake. I never took the time to verify the proof of these stones, or of Cabrera's words. To me, there was something about Dr. Cabrera that was trustworthy. My heart's wisdom knew that his sacrifices were too grand for his story not to be true. He lost his profession and his family fulfilling his promise to a much larger purpose. Due to his commitment and dedication to sharing the wisdom of these stones, many people believe that the history of our planet (and of humanity) needs to be reevaluated. Perhaps this is why many people want to disprove Cabrera and these stones—it is much easier to live life as we currently know and understand it, and these stones suggest that there is more to the history and future of life and our planet than our current understanding of it. Personally, I feel extremely blessed to have been in Cabrera's presence and to learn about these stones directly from him. He kept his word to the man and the light beings, and he lived the rest of his life dedicated to sharing his sacred work. Sometimes this is all we need—a man of integrity whose actions match his words, just like my own father taught me. To me, this is more than enough "proof."

SHAMANIC JOURNEY

TO THE CAVE OF ICA STONES

Guided by Vera Lopez

It's time to take a deep inner journey. Breathing in through your nose and out through your mouth, I invite you to close your eyes. Allow your heart to open and feel your spirit fly out from your heart space and into the sky above you. Your spirit flies faster, further, and higher through space and time, and you intuitively know that you are journeying to the sacred lands of Peru.

A beam of light rises in the sky and you fly to it. This beam of light is inviting you to go down into the sacred land of the Andes. As you soar downward you notice that you are not far from the coast, and yet you also see a desert land. This union of desert and sea is truly unique. You find your spirit landing upon the Earth and you walk onto the home that was once an ancient civilization.

You walk further into this land and discover a cave. You enter this cave and find it filled with stones of all shapes and sizes. You go deeper into the cave and pick up a medium-size stone, flipping it over and finding it to have on it unique symbols and images. You flip over another stone and another to discover that each stone holds a different set of symbols and images, almost as if each stone holds a story or captures a piece within time.

You are in the cave of Ica stones and these stones tell the stories of the past, the present, and the future. This cave is an ancient library of knowledge and wisdom, and of prophecy. You continue walking around the cave examining each of the different stones and their markings, and you begin to realize that you are not alone. You feel a presence within the cave. You pause and look around you, and as you do so you see these beings of light begin to emerge from the larger stones that are deeper within the cave. These beings have a deep and peaceful presence, and they welcome you to explore this ancient cave and library of stones.

One of the light beings approaches you. It knows your name, and it introduces itself as a plasma being. You bow to this being in acknowledgment and appreciation for being allowed access into this magical and mysterious place. This light being telepathically communicates with you, and he encourages you to find a question for yourself—what mysteries of the world and universe are you seeking to know?

You take a deep breath in through your nose and exhale fully through your mouth. Take a moment to drop into your heart and find your question. What area of your life can you receive clarity and guidance on?

You find your question and hold it in your mind—telepathically reaching out to the being of light. This being receives your question and hands you an Ica stone. You examine the stone—what do you see? Take note of the size of the stone and the symbols and engravings upon it.

This stone and its images have a message for you—a story and pieces of wisdom from the past, the present, and the future. Use your breath to connect with these energies and drop into this stone's specific mysteries as they pertain to your life at this time.

Take a deep breath. And exhale fully. You acknowledge and give thanks to these beings of light for their presence and wisdom. You send your appreciation to the cave and to the stones, and once again thank the beings of light for being the guardians of this ancient library of knowledge and wisdom.

You breathe deeply and leave the cave. Your spirit soars high into the sky, and you carry with you your stone and the wisdom you received from this experience within the cave. Your spirit soars back into your physical reality and you find your body. You breathe in and exhale fully, feeling yourself return back into this time, space, and dimension. Before you fully awake, place your sacred Ica stone on your altar, knowing it is there to reveal deep levels of answers to the question you have asked. Wiggle your fingers and toes. Breathe deeply, and feel yourself return and open your eyes.

Take some time to journal and reflect about your journey. Record your experiences.

PART 3

PREPARING FOR A SACRED JOURNEY TO PERU

PREPARATION

*Physical, Mental, Emotional,
and Spiritual Facets*

PEOPLE OFTEN REFER TO PERU AS ANOTHER PLANET—the ancient temples, the energy of the ceke or ley lines, the high vibrational Quechua language, and of course, the altitudes and strenuous hiking all contribute to this otherworldly experience. Whether you physically travel to Peru or travel there on the astral plane by doing inner shamanic work, this journey is not intended to be taken lightly.

We know that the calling to journey to Peru, and the calling to experience the power of its ancient temples, is louder now than it has ever been before. It has been prophesied that the Condor of the South and the Eagle of the North must fly together so the children of the Earth can awaken. The prophecy is not limited to those living within South America and North America, rather it is a prophecy for everyone upon the Earth. This prophecy speaks to one of the greatest Andean mysteries—the union of the mind and the heart—it's speaking into the awakening of the heart's wisdom.

We also know that, for many reasons, it is not always possible for everyone who is feeling the call to journey to Peru to physically do so. We hope that this book—the teachings and the shamanic journeys shared within these pages—can assist you in accessing the mysteries of the land and experiencing the blessings of Peru's temples and the paqos' medicine. To those wishing to go deeper in their journey with these ancient mysteries, I suggest that you consider experiencing the Andean Mystery School. I formed this mystery school and invited special guest teachers, including Don Wilbert and our Q'eros paqos Don Francisco and Don Pascual. These wisdom keepers will join us in different virtual ceremonies and initiations that will support us in experiencing the ancient mysteries of the Andes. The Andean Mystery School is an online experience that serves as a portal in which we are able to spiritually and energetically connect to Peru and the mysteries within this holy land (see "Resources" on page 177 for more information). We created this virtual mystery school in part to support those wishing to go deep in their preparation prior to physical travel to the Andes, but we especially designed this online offering to support those desiring to experience the mysteries of Peru without physically traveling there. As the old proverb says: If the mountain will not come to Mahomet, Mahomet must go to the mountain.

In either case, preparations made before your journey can greatly support your unique transformative process. As soon as you feel the call to journey to Peru and you make the commitment to yourself and/or a group, the high vibrational energies of this land begin working with you, and it's time for you to prepare. When doing so it's important to take into consideration the different facets of your being. Your mental, emotional, physical, and spiritual bodies will respond to and receive the high vibrations of Peru differently. For example, those who are traveling physically to Peru may experience a strong physical reaction to the high altitude and can become quite ill. Others, including some who travel shamanically, experience deep emotional release, spiritual purification, and profound altered states of consciousness. And some people experience all of these possible experiences. So it's important to prepare each facet of your being before journeying into these higher vibrations.

When we look at preparing the physical body for Peru, it's important to make sure that our bodies are healthy, fit, and equipped to experience a thinner oxygen level and strenuous hiking. Before traveling to Peru, I encourage journeyers to do regular walks and/or other types of cardio-strengthening exercises. It's not to say that you must be super fit to qualify for a trip to Peru. I have guided individuals with various states of physical health—some with excellent physical fitness and others who are not in the best of shape—and none of them missed a bit of the journey due to physical restrictions. However, preparing your physical body will support you in the long run.

In addition to walking, running, and/or biking more, I encourage journeyers to pay attention to their diet and to be mindful of their food choices. The Inca were primarily vegetarian, but today Peruvian society accommodates a wide range of diets. Most Peruvians eat meat, unless they are farmers and/or are living on a limited budget, then their diet mainly consists of vegetables. Because of the large variety of vegetables available, the amount of vegetarian diets is growing within modern-day Peru. Peruvian is actually the second largest cuisine on Earth—the first being Chinese. Lima is well regarded for its gourmet food tours, and Cuzco is also home to several fine-dining establishments. When our groups travel to Aguas Calientes, we eat at one of the best restaurants in Peru—Indio Feliz, which offers a French-Peruvian cuisine. While modern-day Peru can accommodate a wide variety of diets and meal plans, I encourage my groups to begin incorporating a vegetable-rich diet prior to their journey to Peru. A vegetable-rich diet can support your acclimating to the higher elevation and altitude shift. Upon embarking on a journey to Peru, I also encourage and recommend journeyers to actively do their inner work—preparing their mental, emotional, and spiritual bodies for a life-changing adventure.

When we journey to Peru either physically or shamanically, we can experience deep processes that shift how our mental, emotional, and spiritual bodies engage with the world and its many realms. For example, I remember the time I visited my friend Peter Schneider in Lima. Peter was a researcher studying the mysteries of Markawasi—a majestic plateau suspended in an Andean mountain range that overlooks the Rimac River. Markawasi is a curious site that is known for its mysterious shapes of human faces and animals found within granite rock. I have never been to Markawasi in person, but that morning Peter was seated at his dining room table and he was showing me his photo slideshow of Markawasi. During Peter's showing, his telephone rang and he excused himself to go answer it. I continued to go through his slide-show. The next thing I know I am in Markawasi wandering around and exploring the different shapes within the granite stones. This experience was surreal, and it felt like a dream. I do not recall how long I was in Markawasi, but the next thing I remember is that Peter had returned from his phone call and he was gently waking me up. I woke up astonished and shared with him my experience in Markawasi. Peter stared at me with wide eyes and said that he believed me. He encouraged me to go look at my face in the bathroom. When I did, I discovered that my face had become sunburned. I must note that my face was not sunburned before my experience in Markawasi, but as I learned shortly after, when one astral projects—sending his or her spirit to another location or dimension—it is possible for the physical body to experience the place as if it is physically there. I had astral projected to Markawasi and my face received a sunburn because of this experience! This is an example of how the physicality of a highly charged place—like Peru—can affect the physical body. Not only does Peru influence and impact the physical body but it also makes shifts within one's energetic field, causing accelerated spiritual growth and personal transformations to occur. As mentioned before, Peru truly is another planet.

You will be provided with the opportunity to experience direct initiations and transformative ceremonies with the Q'eros paqos (the Andean shamans). Through these transformative processes and experiences, you are able to enter into a portal of healing and awakening where you may find yourself releasing outdated programing, heavy emotions, and old ego identities.

In preparing for your journey to Peru, I encourage you to actively begin examining your own life and see what areas of it are ready for transformation. Actively staying on top of, and/or engaged with, your inner realms can greatly support your transformative process. Over the years I have witnessed many people have a gentle yet powerful experience within Peru. I have also witnessed and held space for many individuals who struggled and had a challenging time during their journey to Peru. As I have reflected upon these contrasting experiences, I have come to understand that Peru itself is life-changing. The land is filled with vortexes and highly charged places of power. Visiting this land and experiencing the initiations of the sacred sites will bring stuff up—old wounds for healing, physical detox and cleansing, and spiritual revelations. This is why I recommend that those embarking on a journey to Peru stay attuned to their inner work and their own transformational process. Preparing the body, mind, and spirit allows you to enter Peru and gently receive the medicine of this sacred land. Not doing your inner work or personal healing can result in an intense experience for body, mind, and spirit. I have come to the realization that as individuals do their inner work and personal healing, they keep their energetic bodies and channels open and cleared of unresolved issues. This allows them to enter the vibrational field of Peru with little to no repercussions. For those that do not prepare themselves, they usually experience some sort of physical, emotional, and spiritual detox—and it can be quite intense. We cannot avoid doing our inner work. We may not know what it is we need to work on or how it will manifest, but in your preparation for Peru it is important to utilize your spiritual tools and practices, which will support you in raising your vibration.

I highly recommend preparing yourself prior to your journey. Increase your personal self-care regimen—eat well, sleep well, and move your physical body. In addition, set aside time to meditate and practice other spiritual practices—and formulate an intention for your journey within your mind and heart. All of these recommendations will support you in preparing for Peru. And in preparing for Peru you are actually attuning yourself to the vibrational field of Peru itself.

ANSWERING THE CALL TO PERU

Initiations and Gargoyles at the Gate

The invitation that the spirits have for us is to always empty our vessels—to clear our physical, mental, emotional, and spiritual bodies of blockages that keep us from fully embodying love. When we make a commitment to experience a spiritual pilgrimage to a high sacred place, our lives will change.

When we look at this journey as if we are walking upon a spiral path and we are beginning in the center of the labyrinth and then extending our journey outward, we start in gratitude. We start by being grateful to the spirits who have invited us to take this sacred journey. We are grateful for the spirits who have created and supported all the alignments that have made it possible to be called to and journey to Peru.

The stories I have heard over the past thirty years of people being called to Peru are miraculous. What I have found is that the moment people say "yes!" to the call, the spirits of Peru begin to work to support and create the alignment just because that person has made the commitment. For those who intend to travel physically to Peru, most have no idea how the journey is going to manifest financially, in terms of work, in terms of family, or in terms of health, but again, once the commitment is made, the spirits begin to work on their behalf to facilitate the trip.

And in some cases, people experience the opposite—as soon as they say yes, they experience all sorts of blocks. But these blocks are somehow a test for these people to go through to see how committed they are to actually undergoing this journey. Peru can be such an important initiation in our lives that sometimes our ego minds can sabotage our soul's commitment. It can create all of these things to second-guess our soul's commitment.

For some people the journey up to Peru is smooth, and they begin to open up to the energies: they have dreams and magic begins to unfold in their life as they expand into the mysteries and energies of this ancient land. And others experience contraction and resistance. In the end, those who carry through on their commitment move past the gargoyles at the gate and enter the sacred lands of Peru. Once they are in these ancient lands they still fly high on the magic of these energies.

For those who encountered more resistance and blockages, when they get to Peru they surrender; they feel the relief of finally having made the journey. They have made it through all the tests because their initiation began before they arrived in Peru. Once you've made it there, you have already undergone deep spiritual preparation and initiation. The moment you say yes to Peru, your journey begins.

The Story of My Name of Power—
and a Gargoyle at the Gate

Everything that we cannot comprehend or explain enters the category of the sacred mysteries. You know those things we could make up, yet they happen anyway? Some call them coincidences while others know that they are synchronicities—alignments with the flow of the universe. Throughout my years, I have come to understand that the magic of Spirit is always behind these synchronicities.

Peru has an infinite sea of synchronistic possibilities, and I've had the opportunity to directly experience many of these mysterious alignments, one of which I wish to share in the story below.

A few years after I started leading journeys to Peru, I was honored with a medicine name by one of my Peruvian spiritual teachers, Kucho. A powerful medicine man, Kucho is respected for his vast authority within the ancient mysteries of Machu Picchu. He journeyed alongside me and one of my groups, and during this journey he provided me and several others within our group with a medicine name—a name of power that an individual can call upon, grow into, and embody that reflects the essence of his or her spirit.

Our group was sitting in a circle when Kucho started to go around and channel a medicine name for each person. When my turn came to receive a name, Kucho turned to me and named me Coyarimac. He explained that *coya* is Quechua for "queen, wife, and sister of the Inca." *Rimac* means "the one who speaks" or "the speaker." When the words *coya* and *rimac* come together they translate to mean "the one who carries power in her words."

I took this name to heart and felt a huge responsibility to live up to it. To me, my new name was inviting me to step up and begin to choose my words wisely and with intention. Kucho later shared with me that he felt I was already operating from this level of power but encouraged me to lean ever more into this energy and power within myself. I knew this to be true as I made a commitment to myself when I began to teach spiritual and metaphysical subjects: I would always walk my talk, and if I could not apply a teaching or a subject within my own life than I could never attempt to teach it.

I must admit that when I received this name of power I felt that a piece changed within me. I wondered how I could respectfully carry this energy and live up to the name's responsibility, while also staying humble. I meditated on this and came to understand that this quandary was a lesson of the name itself, and it was one that I continued to grow into over time.

A few years after I received the name Coyarimac I was facilitating another amazing group. Most of the participants had journeyed from Hawaii to Peru to experience and connect with the ancient Andean mysteries. Within this group, I had the privilege of having Kahili, a kahuna, or Hawaiian medicine man, and his wife, Antoinette, journey alongside me. Together, these planetary change agents and I did beautiful work building energetic bridges between the land of Peru and the holy islands of Hawaii. We called upon their gods and goddesses as well as the Apus of Peru, and we asked for unity to cultivate within our tribes. We asked for assistance in awakening Mother Earth's children so that each person would know his or her sacred purpose and be strong enough to carry it out into the world.

As offerings we planted sacred seeds from Hawaii in the sacred lands of Peru. This was a ritual and ceremony that everyone in our group did and it was a beautiful fusion of these two ancient cultures. Kahili was an incredible human being and a true kahuna. I learned that his family initiated the healing practices of lomilomi. During this journey I had a lomilomi session with him. I have never experienced healing hands quite like his. His touch not only unblocked every energetic point in my body, but I also remember my astral body floating above us and receiving medicine from the Hawaiian ancestors.

Antoinette, Kahili's wife, was a hula master. During our journey she performed hula ceremonies in honor of the Apus. Our group collectively felt the response of the mountains as she chanted and danced. During Antoinette's ceremony Kahili played his ukulele, and through their ceremonial union we all entered an enchanted trancelike state.

On this particular journey, our group was scheduled for a special sunrise ceremony in Machu Picchu. Both Kahili and Antoinette had traveled from Hawaii to offer their best ceremonious contributions to the sacred site of Machu Picchu during the sunrise. Antoinette had prepared a special and sacred hula dance to honor Taita Inti, Grandfather Sun of the Andean nation. This dance would also honor the Apus of Machu Picchu, Huayna Picchu, and Putucusi.

As we entered the gates of Machu Picchu, we all had a lot of anticipation within our hearts; we were all eager and excited to journey and watch the sunrise within these ancient and magical ruins. But as we entered, one of the guards stopped us and said that Kahili could not bring his ukulele into Machu Picchu; he would have to leave his instrument in storage or not enter at all.

Kahili turned to me and said, "Vera, I cannot enter without my ukulele. It is a family treasure and I go nowhere without it. I accept that I cannot play the ukulele within Machu Picchu, but I cannot enter and leave it here in storage."

We all felt a deep hurt within our hearts because of this turn of events. For a moment I felt absolutely powerless, but I could not and would not let that stop us from entering. Deep within my core I knew the importance of this moment and I knew the sacrifices that Kahili and Antoinette had made to be at Machu Picchu for the sunrise.

I asked my tour guide to enter Machu Picchu with the rest of our group, and I stayed at the gate with Kahili and Antoinette. At this point it was about five o'clock in the morning and I knew that the supervisor for the Machu Picchu guards was still asleep. I tried my best to explain to the guard that this was an important and sacred instrument. I promised the guard that Kahili would not play the ukulele within the site but explained that he could not leave it behind in storage. The guard did not budge and continued to deny us entrance into Machu Picchu.

At this point I asked to speak to his supervisor. The guard told me that would not be possible because his supervisor was still sleeping. I smiled at the guard and told him that we could go and wake him if he did not feel comfortable doing so. We demanded to speak with his supervisor and insisted upon our right to do so. This lasted for several minutes—back and forth, back and forth—until the guard finally left the gate to wake his supervisor.

As we waited for the guard to return with his supervisor, I prepared myself to encounter a man who would not be happy at being woken up, but I had to try every honest way I knew to make it possible for Kahili and Antoinette to enter with their ukulele.

The supervisor came and he was half awake, as I expected. To this day, I am not sure what I said or how I spoke to the supervisor; all I know is that within minutes Kahili, Antoinette, and I were allowed access into Machu Picchu with Kahili's ukulele. We were all so excited, we screamed with joy as we entered! We rushed through the gate and into the ruins just as the sun was rising over the mountains.

At that exact moment, Kahili turned to me and said, "Vera, you are the ManaLeo."

I stopped and asked him for the meaning of ManaLeo.

Kahili explained, "*Mana* is the spiritual energy of power and strength. *Leo* is the voice. When these words come together, they mean 'the one who carries power within their words.'"

I was stunned! Here I was again in Machu Picchu receiving yet another name with the same essence, the same meaning, and the same vibration. How could this be happening, I thought to myself? Two medicine men—one from Peru and one from Hawaii—giving me the same spiritual name; how was this possible?

I was overwhelmed with honor to receive this name of power yet again. I knew that the spirits were making sure I would never forget the gifts they had given me, and I knew that the guard at the gate of Machu Picchu was my personal "gargoyle at the gate" challenging me to own this energy within myself and move fully into the initiation of my spiritual names: Coyarimac and ManaLeo. While I have not changed my name to either of these names, I carry the essence, the responsibility, and the energy of both names within my heart. I use both of these names of power for the good of all.

᚛᚜

THE ILL WINDS AND THE HUAYRURO BEADS

If you are physically traveling to Peru, it's important for you to stay grounded and connected to the Earth. Some say that the high altitude is what causes us to become ungrounded. Others say that they believe Peru to be closer to the heavens and the stars, and these high frequencies are what unground us. Regardless of the cause, journeying to Peru can be activating, and it is important for all who go to have a strong, stable, and secure root chakra. When traveling to different sacred sites around the world, it is also important to acknowledge the customs and practices of their different cultures, which include not only modern-day traditions, but also the ancient shamanic practices found throughout these lands.

If you are taking a spiritual pilgrimage to a sacred site such as Peru, and you are journeying with a mystical eye, or a shamanic perspective, then it is important to remember that there are spirits still roaming these ancient lands. Perhaps there are angels, devas, or other spirits and energies connected and very much alive in this land. So it is important to remain grounded and also protected throughout your journey.

One such story that comes to mind is the day our group traveled to the village of Pisac. One this day, half of our group wanted to hike along the great winding trails through the high mountains to see the place where the ancient astrologers and priests lived—the Incan ruins—and the other half of our group wanted to remain in the village and shop at the local markets found throughout Pisac. Vera and I remained in the village with those who wished to go shopping, and a couple of our experienced tour guides guided the other half of our group to the Incan ruins.

The Incan ruins were home to the mystics and seers of Pisac. These wise medicine men and women knew how to read the stars and watch for the seasons. They told the farmers in the villages below when to plant the crops and when to harvest the crops. These wise men and women were in communion with nature and the cycles of life, and they shared these mysteries with the villagers below so that life might continue to flow harmoniously.

When the invaders and intruders came to Peru from other countries, the foreigners tore down these structures and enslaved these mystical people who were the communication bridge between this world and the next. Because of the tragedies and aggressive force imprinted upon this land, some say and believe that the spirits of wise beings still reside in these mountains as the Ill Winds—the winds that will sweep you up and take you away to the otherworlds and other realms.

On our journey to Pisac, a young man who was a part of our group decided to hike with the other group members to the Incan ruins. Rather than staying as a pack, which Vera and I both encourage, this young man decided to venture off into the high mountains by himself. While he was separate from the rest of the group, the tour guides were still able to keep an eye on him and watch him from a distance. Little did they know that, at the time, this young man was having a deep and powerful visionary experience.

As the hike was coming to a close and the group was preparing to make their way back down the mountain, the guides tried to bring this young man back together with the rest of the group. As they discovered, he was deep into himself and experiencing an enmeshment with the otherworld. As the guides attempted to bring him down the mountain, they discovered that he had been possessed by the Ill Winds. This young man had become ungrounded and he was overtaken by these wandering spirits. A strong part of him did not want to leave the mountain. He felt that he belonged on this mountain. He said that the mountaintop was his home, and that he was supposed to stay there for the remainder of his life.

Now, Vera and I were already in the village of Pisac. Our guides, with our group on the mountain, had sent word ahead that this young man was in a highly expanded state of consciousness, and that he was having some anxiety and resistance about coming down from the mountaintop. He felt as if it were his life's mission to remain on top of this mountain and bring back the old ways, which had been forgotten and obliterated by the sands of time.

The guides were eventually able to bring this young man down from the mountain and back into the village of Pisac, where he rejoined Vera and me. He sat between us on a bench just outside of a café, facing the main streets and busy square of Pisac. When he returned to us, Vera and I sat on either side of him and encouraged him to take deep breaths in and out, grounding him back into his body. His eyes were dilated, his body was shaking, and he was laughing. Both Vera and I knew that he was not present in this world. We put our hands on his heart and we encouraged him to breathe into his body, pulling his spirit back into his physical form.

At this exact moment, an elderly woman came walking up to us from off the streets. She was a local woman who was hunched over from carrying straw and bricks on her back. She was bent almost double yet didn't seem to be in any pain. Her skin was wrinkled and brown. She had a toothless smile and bright eyes. She didn't speak any English, but she walked over to us and placed her hand on this young man's chest and she started to whisper a foreign chant in his ear.

"Wire, Wire, Wire, Wire!" chanted the woman.

Vera, who can understand the language spoken by the natives, translated and said that this woman was chanting to the god Wire. Wire is the god who can remove the Ill Winds—the winds and spirits that live among the high mountaintops, who possess ungrounded individuals and take them away to the spirit worlds. Vera said that some natives were fearful of these spirits, but the elders and wiser locals knew that they were those of their ancestors who had come to deliver a message from the other side.

This elderly woman continued to work with this young man. Vera and I also continued to encourage him to breathe. The elderly woman pulled out a bundle of herbs and ran it under his nose and around his body, as if she were smudging his physical and energetic bodies. Within moments of smelling these herbs, he began to return. His eyes came back to a normal appearance, his breathing steadied, and he began to fully enter back into his body.

When the elderly woman recognized that he was back from the otherworld and fully in this dimension, she gave him a set of huayruro beads for protection and grounding. These are beads that the people commonly wear for good luck. As he began to fully return, he started to tell Vera and me about his altered experience on the other side. It was clear that he was deeply altered by this experience. In the end, this was a deeply powerful and shamanic experience for us all.

Whenever you go to sacred sites or high vibrational places it is of the utmost importance to journey prepared. Vera and I both know this after facilitating groups for several decades. It is important to be prepared in a practical way—having enough water, snacks, and appropriate clothing so that you can stay grounded in your body. But it is also important to stay energetically protected and shielded from strong influential energies, especially if you are an open, vulnerable, and mystical person. If you subscribe to being one of these types of people (open, vulnerable, and mystical) then it is probably best that you do not journey these lands alone.

Go with a group and stay close to your tour guides, who have grown up on this land. There are tremendous energies and vortexes throughout the world and these ancient spirits still reside within them and call these places home. Whether you visit the natural scenery or the ancient temples, these spirits are still wandering the land, and they can connect with you. Be honoring of inner and outer guidance and these sacred energies—while humbly practicing being grounded. Offering a sincere prayer asking for permission and calling in protection on all levels will connect you in a good way to the guardian spirits of the land and open you to your own innate wisdom and the shaman within yourself.

Peru is a vortex, and in preparing yourself beforehand you don't need to do too much; just allow the codes of light to come in through your breath. When you journey to Peru, you are in a portal; you are in a high multidimensional frequency. Peru is really powerful. Peru is truly one of the most sacred places on Earth.

SHARING

Shamanic Stories from Peru

IN THIS CHAPTER WE WILL HEAR compelling stories from some of the people who have heard and answered the call to journey to Peru. Each one contains a great deal of wisdom and shares a very special message with us.

Journey to Peru
Ruth Kellogg

I booked my trip for October 2018 in September 2017. Little did I know that this trip and all its components would play a powerful role in a healing I did not know I would need.

In July of 2017 my son had a psychotic break. If you've ever had to watch someone you love come apart before your eyes you can relate to how much helplessness and deep pain this can cause in your whole body and being. In my search, in the way of the shamanic tradition and a recognition that we are all one, I began to ask questions and find answers. The biggest question for me was, What is it in this experience with my son that I am being asked to heal in me?

By the time October rolled around, I had begun to intellectually understand what my soul might be attempting to show me. However, there were so many aspects of my Peruvian trip that brought my understanding to a physical/visceral level and truly allowed me to heal my deep-heart, whole-body pain around the loss of a son I thought I knew.

In Peru, from day one we were introduced, through ceremony, to the paqos who would accompany us to sacred sites to share their wisdom and healing. The philosophy of this culture incorporates all living and nonliving aspects in and on the Earth—as well as the cosmos—as part of a whole, living, breathing integrated system. I am/we are all part of that intelligently orchestrated system. My experience was most personal but was in the context of this wholeness.

Shamanic Breathwork was part of our protocol. When we experienced it on our second day I was given, inside of this journey, knowledge about how to use my perception to see my experience with my son through a close-up lens, or the lens my soul might use as an awareness looking in from the cosmos herself. As my higher self or inside journey guide took my awareness into my bodily close-up experience and then out to the experience of mere awareness being aware of itself, I began to realize that I had a choice. My choice pertained to how I wanted to live my experience of life here on Earth, not only as it related to my son but as it related to all of life. It was like breathing room into my body and beforehand, I'd had no idea of this capacity. This extra "breathing" room gave me much to ponder about who I am and how I fit as this tiny yet mighty particle in the whole of life. There is so much freedom there!

As we continued through the week, being in Peru and living in the timeless consciousness that had shaped the indigenous people and their great love for and trust in the cosmic energies, I found my deeper self coming into a realization of how we are all supported. I am here now, in this particular suit of skin. My awareness can see itself trapped, if you will, inside this skin. I can also untrap my awareness and use it to know that my true home is within the awareness of all that is. To choose to know myself as an awareness that can blend with all of life, and be inside of a leaf, or a mountain, or a mountain stream, is our gift as a human with awareness. I need not attach my awareness and define myself as simply this singular human having a human painful experience. I always have a choice.

By the end of the week, my turn for a personal healing with Paqo Francisco came around. In that short hour, he was able to pull from my physical form all the cellular pain I had been holding since those moments in early July when I felt the searing pain of my whole world being torn apart. This pain has not returned. Paqo knew his role in transformation and my experience throughout the week allowed me to accept the possibility of the miracle of this healing. The fact that

I was given the eyes of the cosmos—the ability to see the larger picture—was a bonus that has helped me in the practice of my life ever since my trip; for that I am deeply grateful.

In those days of deep pain in early July, I had said to God, or the cosmos: "If love heals, show me the love that will heal my son! Teach me that! I want to know that love!" In the months since having made that request, I have been supported and shown a road I did not expect to travel. I thought I would be learning to love and heal my son and accept him. While that is true, the greater learning has been in leaning into the all-encompassing direct principle of love— an intelligent orchestration that can be surrendered to when we realize we are awareness experiencing its self, which is literally another plane of existence.

The gentle, loving people and the cosmic traditions of Peru have played a role in helping me be immersed in their way of life, to see the value of going slower, incorporating the intelligent love and support that lives within and all around us. The very history of these people draws upon this universal wisdom. However, I have free will, so I may partner with cosmic perception and the healing capacity for acceptance and self-acceptance—an acceptance of all of life no matter how it fits or does not fit into my cultural roles and rules.

It is my choice to choose to live from this amazing plane of existence. As Star Wolf says, "Dark, light—no difference." Vera, Star Wolf, and two other journeyers—Nikólaus and Jasin—held a most amazing container for transformation within the consciousness of the Andes and all that consciousness brings to us humans; divine intelligence does the rest! Deep gratitude to you and all of life!

The Divine Feminine Calling
Michael Mammina

Ever since I was a young child, an image of a mountain would appear in my mind, and I had no idea what exactly it represented. As life went on, I lost sight of that mountain until one day I saw a book called Out on a Limb by Shirley MacLaine and read through it, knowing that this place she described was somewhere I needed to visit in my lifetime.

Putting aside all those thoughts and continuing with life, I met a woman named Vera Lopez at a spiritual center in Chicago. We were both members of *this church, Unity of Chicago, and she was working with the minister organizing a journey to Peru. Little did I know that standing in front of me was one of my greatest teachers and a mirror for a life I was about to step into. She described an enchanted place called Machu Picchu and told me that she had received a message for me to join the group and take the trip with our church. Because of the busyness of my life, I resisted and kept putting it off until she kept persisting and telling me how important it was for me to visit there as there was a critical message and lesson for me. Being a skeptic, quite honestly, I didn't believe her and thought, wow, this woman is a fantastic marketer!*

Forty-three people from the center did go on the trip with Vera that year. When they returned they had nothing but amazing stories to share, and the following year Vera approached me again. She told me that the message she received was still strong and calling me, I needed to join her on her next journey. I decided it was time and made plans to join a group of eight people for what would be one of the essential journeys of my life.

That first trip to Peru was truly magical; all of the temples and sacred sites that we visited opened my heart with each step I took. One very sacred place of my transformation and awakening was an ancient planting ruin called Moray, otherwise known as the Womb of the Mother. Its wide concentric circles, used for planting and nourishment, form a womb shape that descends deep into the ground. And with every layer that you climb farther into it, there is a feeling of energy and rebirth. It was a feeling I had never experienced, and I was unaware of what was happening to me. Leaving there, feeling a deep sense of love, I didn't realize that it was actually all in preparation for what was about to happen next.

When we finally reached Machu Picchu, I fell to my knees, knowing that there was a love there that I had never quite felt before; that love was the love of Pachamama, the Divine Mother. Each moment that I walked on that sacred ground peeled back another layer of pain or struggle I had experienced in my life, allowing me to enter into a dimension like none other. I felt the deep connection and healing love of Mother Earth, the love of Mother Killa, the love of Mother Coca Leaf, and the love of Mother Ayahuasca. The Divine Feminine embraced me and healed me at depths within my heart I was not aware were possible. When it was time to leave for the last time, and after receiving so many powerful blessings, they had to pull me off the mountain in tears. When I turned for the final look, I heard the mountain say, "bring my children back to me," and that's precisely what I did for the next seven years. I was blessed to return to Machu Picchu for the next seven years and bring the Children of the Sun back to the Mother. Every time Vera returned to Machu Picchu, I was right by her side supporting and helping in any way I could, while the love of a Mother showered countless people. Each time, receiving more and more love and healing for myself as well.

Midway through this seven-year journey, my biological mother developed Alzheimer's and due to her confusion it was no longer possible for me to embrace her or hold her. On our next trip to Machu Picchu I heard her soul speaking to me on the mountain, telling me that she was fine, that even though she couldn't talk to me any longer her love for me would never end—and that the love I feel in Machu Picchu is truly her love as well. Naturally, this gave me great comfort, and after she transitioned from her body I created a small altar in her honor, hidden away on Machu Picchu. Each day that I feel the need for that special love, that love of the Mother, Mother Earth, and my mother, I can return to Machu Picchu in my mind, knowing that it's always there to access—not just for me but for everyone to feel her loving embrace.

With Vera as my guide and teacher, I have been blessed to visit many sacred places. Brazil, France, and Spain each held a spiritual exploration and journey where I was touched by the Mother once again and experienced the power and the beauty of the Divine Feminine. This is a gift that I almost passed up; I am eternally grateful that I took that first step to Peru.

See with New Eyes
Candace Stack

As I ponder my miraculous experience in Machu Picchu, there are so many real, tangible changes and realizations that occurred there. I believe that my most valuable revelation came to me as I returned to my life in the workplace, following my trip to Machu Picchu.

Before the journey to Peru, I was blasted with some unbelievably difficult news: at my school, the position of my full-time helper and aide would be cut due to budget cuts. Thus I would be required to carry the same workload, but with half the manpower. It would just be me! As a teacher-librarian in a middle school, I had a full teaching load and was also responsible for the total functioning of the media center and library. I took this news with me to Peru and prayed for a miracle.

While on the Peruvian journey, I felt constantly amazed and was blessed with many daily experiences. These included meeting sacred shamans, seeing my first llamas (my favorite), enjoying fellow travelers, experiencing local culture, meeting the beautiful Incan families and children, and being enfolded by Vera's sweet and nurturing guidance.

One of the trip's highlights was to celebrate the opening of the first school in a remote Peruvian mountain village. Our Unity Church members had collected supplies and we were to help with the opening of this new school. I couldn't have dreamed that this experience would shift my entire life. These children came to the school opening with wide eyes, gratitude, and absolute joy. The modest building had no glass in the windows, no electricity, a dirt floor, and few school supplies. Yet the villagers were filled with such gratitude and exuberance that my heart was spilling over.

We brought balloons to celebrate the opening—many of the native children had never ever seen a balloon. They were amazed. Our day with the mountain village school was the highlight of the journey for many of us. It was so beautiful and humbling, so joyous and emotional!

A few weeks later, as I returned home and walked into my school in Illinois, I truly experienced the realization I was waiting for. "I was the lucky one!" My relatively new building featured a beautiful, tall wood beamed ceiling with a Frank Lloyd Wright design. It held twenty thousand books for students and teachers, provided eight big screen computers, and it surrounded us with heat and air-conditioning aplenty—and so much more. In comparison, those Peruvian children with their modest building with its dirt floor felt that they had been given a castle, the Taj Mahal.

It was then that I realized I truly worked in a facility that was like the Taj Mahal, with every modern creature comfort and technology. My thought was How dare I feel sorry for myself for losing my helper! I certainly had been given a gift. I have always loved teaching, but now I renewed my commitment to teach my students with more fervor and appreciation. Gratitude, gratitude, gratitude would be my daily lesson and I would be forever changed. Those Peruvian children's angel faces are locked in my heart. Their sweet, innocent joy and amazement are a precious gift that I wish all of humanity could experience!

Many of us are given so much! Yet we take this for granted. I was reminded of the things that truly matter, but with new eyes and a new heart, courtesy of the universe.

The Divine Embrace of Pachamama
Dr. Lucille Necas

I'm not one to be riveted by posters, but this one stopped me in my tracks.

There in the foyer of the Grail Springs Wellness Retreat in Bancroft, Ontario, Canada, I stood transfixed in front of the picture of Machu Picchu. It was advertising a spiritual journey to Peru with a tour company called Spirits of the Earth. In that moment it was as if the energy of a mountain entered every cell of my being and made it clear that I had no choice but to go.

At the time, I was a practicing psychiatrist in Toronto, Canada, entering a completely new chapter of my life. My mother had died and my grief was transmuting into a hunger to spread my wings and fly. Officially an orphan, I was now free to be and do exactly what my heart desired. My heart had led me to the magical "grail" which, for a time, became like a home away from home, and the "grail" led me to Pachamama.

The tour was led by shaman and founder of Spirits of the Earth Vera Lopez, as well as two other seasoned shamans and spiritual guides. I was journeying into a depth of spiritual connection with myself that I had only scratched the surface of before.

There are power spots on this planet that I've visited or heard of but none so compelling and palpable for me as Peru. I find it difficult to describe. Words cannot convey the profound relationship I feel with this realm that lies half a world away.

I will describe only a few highlights, given that I experienced so many magical moments.

At the airport in Cuzco, I disembarked and made a beeline for the public washroom. Standing in the lineup, I noticed the most loving, bliss-inducing energy start working its way up from the floor and through my entire body. It felt as if it had a maternal consciousness. I got it—"Pachamama" became totally real to me in that moment. And she accompanied me during the entire journey.

Ascending with the group up to the entrance of Machu Picchu, Vera asked us to close our eyes and link hands as she guided us along a narrow path. At the top of the climb she instructed us to open our eyes to our first view of the breathtaking grandeur of this otherworldly realm. Despite hordes of tourists, there was an ethereal calm and the air seemed alive with a shimmering, effervescent light. I could have sprouted wings and flown like an Andean condor out over the scene. I was utterly exhilarated.

I have never been drawn to creating stories of a past reincarnation. The experience was so vast, transformative, and mysterious that locking it all into a story would be to diminish the power of it. I embrace it all in the raw state that's become embedded in my DNA.

One afternoon, after the rest of our group had left the site, I was blessed with a private tour led by Vera and another guide, the behind-the-scenes, unofficial tour that you can't get with the official guides. I don't know what led me to stay behind, other than my heart was captivated and searching for something.

From the moment I first laid eyes on the Machu Picchu vista, my gaze was drawn to a small, sugar-loaf-shaped mountain across the river from the site. I was transfixed by it, for it was like the magnetic pull of an attractive stranger. Vera and the other guide explained that it was called Putucusi, which was Quechua for "Happiness Mountain." The indigenous people in the area believed it contained a portal to a magical realm and that it was meant to protect Machu Picchu or Machu Picchu was created to protect it.

Vera instructed me to lean back against a gigantic boulder in the retaining wall of the hill overlooking the mountain and then suggested that I gaze directly at the mountain itself. In so doing I experienced the deepest sense of a loving connection that moved me to my core. I came home to my infinite self in that moment.

Vera and the other guide gave me many gifts of otherworldly experiences that day. I carry them with me in my heart and often bless them both for their wisdom and generosity of spirit. And Putucusi still comes to me from time to time to comfort, soothe, and inspire me to remember who I truly am.

One of the other guides popped up everywhere like a nature spirit, dressed in full indigenous costume and ready to play the role of childlike trickster, wise woman of the mountains, or devout healer. She came to each of us with intuitive messages of what we needed for healing or spiritual connection. In my case, I was to find two stones on my journey wanderings through the Machu Picchu site to take back home with me. They were not to be just any stones picked up haphazardly, but ones that I would somehow recognize. Having never experienced myself as intuitive, I had no idea how I would do this for that entire area was completely strewn with stones.

During a grueling daylong hike up Huayna Picchu, I found them. They quietly and deliberately "announced" themselves to me among all the stones and pebbles along the route. Somehow I sensed a different energy about them. They were about five feet apart and no larger than the palm of my hand. They were filled with granite crystals. One was like a base with small indentations in it and the other was phallic or mountain-shaped and obviously was meant to sit vertically on the base stone. I intuited that they wanted to come home with me. You see, I have no doubt that they have a consciousness.

The other guide confirmed that the stones wanted to come home with me. So now they sit in my office at home—my faithful companions. I seem to be able to balance the mountain stone on its base very easily if it's knocked over, which is a constant inspiration to me to center myself.

Huayna Picchu called out my feminine essence and made me aware of the primordial energy of the priestesses that had performed rituals there. The spirits of the priestesses seemed to be everywhere. They or something otherworldly drew me into a temple, actually a cave, in the side of the mountain. This cave was dedicated to serpents and I knew I had to make my way to its darkest portion where there was a ledge that was part of an entrance to a smaller portion of the cave.

I sat on the ledge looking out toward the cave entrance, which was a small circle of sunlight in the distance. I knew to meditate in what felt like a vast cool depth of silence and darkness. Suddenly I heard a rustling sound behind me to my right; it was moving toward me. Strangely, although my brain was coming up with alarming ideas of what it could be, I was totally calm and certain that nothing would harm me. I then felt a sharp sting in my throat, as if a thin dart had pierced it. There was nothing there. Again I felt absolutely no fear. Again I have no stories of what this was or what it meant but I was left with the sense that something about me had been altered—and would never be the same again.

I've written this description out of love and gratitude for the gift of having unearthed my profound connection to the Earth and to the infinite. Pachamama gave me myself and, along with this, a deep love of humanity and a certainty of *our oneness with this planet and the universal forces that love and guide us. I am hoping that this inspires all who read it to open to the embrace of Pachamama.*

A Journey of Never Being the Same
Jim Hostler

One thing Vera taught me when traveling with her was to not have expectations of what the journey may have in store for you. I have had several profound experiences in my travels with Vera, all of which are diminished when put into words. However, one ceremony stands out above all others and my life is not, nor ever will be, the same because of it.

In June of 2016 I returned to the mystical land of Peru and I was very much in the space of being in the moment, allowing the mysteries to unfold as they did on my previous journeys. I was so ready to be there, back walking in the old streets of the navel of the Earth, Cuzco. I decided to pay a visit to my favorite shaman. When I discovered that he was hosting an ayahuasca ceremony that night, I knew I was to partake in it and so I took the rest of the day to prepare for another transformational journey. It wasn't my first time, but little did I know what lay ahead for me in this upcoming ceremony!

I knew and trusted my shaman brother; again, it wasn't my first time having a ceremony with him. I am so grateful for the words of wisdom Vera shared with me regarding ayahuasca ceremonies. Truly priceless. She advised me to always set an intention with the medicine for "my highest and best good." The ceremony is a dynamic experience, with the great Mother Snake being with you throughout the process, guiding you through each step, each lesson, each dimension.

The time had come to join the small group that was doing the ceremony that evening. We all met with the shaman's assistant and drove away from Cuzco to the shaman's spiritual center located on top of the mountain where Cuzco and the jungle meet. I remember the deep silence of the area and the beauty of the stars as I entered the room where we were having the ceremony. We could all feel the energy of the room, as ceremonies have been held there for years. With excitement for what lay ahead, and in complete trust knowing I was safe, the ceremony began.

Ayahuasca is unique, powerful, and to be respected. You never have the same experience with it. You never know what to expect. This experience, this *ceremony with this ancient medicine, used by the Inca to lead the Empire of the Sun, was to forever transform my life.*

To this day, I can still recall the chant of the shaman. And when I hear it or focus on remembering it, I almost instantly go to another dimension. As I felt the ayahuasca begin its journey in me, initially it was beautiful. But the beauty wasn't going to last. And indeed, it didn't. The purging took me to a depth I had never experienced, ever. I remember thinking, I simply cannot go any further, there is no more of me to give, *and simultaneously knowing I had reached the end of this phase of the journey—the "rewiring," clearing, detoxing, whatever you want to call it, was complete. If there is a "going through hell," I had just completed that journey. After the completion of stage two—the intense detox and rewiring—came what I believe to be the most transformative, powerful, mystical experience of my life.*

The next part of my journey with the Great Serpent has become my most powerful memory of the ceremony. I now began three conversations . . . *at one time. My ego knew it had been discovered and it was screaming in fear. My higher self was there acknowledging the ego and telling me that this was a good thing. And at the deepest part of my beingness, I knew that to be true and became the observer of my ego. The third conversation defies words. The closest I can come is to say that I was talking to God. I was no longer aware of my body, my surroundings, I was completely gone from the physical world. I know what "peace beyond understanding" is, I have experienced it. I know what love is, I have experienced it.*

As time has come between me and the ceremony, I live the experience of what being reborn truly is. My gratitude to Vera lives beyond words: for sharing her wisdom about the ceremony, about how to prepare both physically and mentally for it, and for all the other profound and beautiful experiences I have had while traveling with her. None of it would have been possible without her mastery of guiding sacred journeys.

OPENING THE MESA OF OUR HEARTS

Journey with Snake, Puma, and Condor

SO HERE WE ARE, READY AND WILLING to go deeper within ourselves and together enter the mysteries of Peru—the shamanic mysteries of Peru.

The portal that we have right here in front of us is the portal of our hearts. I want to invite you to breathe in and breathe out, and as you breathe in and breathe out, become aware of your heart as a portal. This multidimensional door has pathways that lead to infinite places, which lead to infinite sacred sites, which lead to infinite realms of consciousness.

Your breathing becomes coherent, and you feel yourself deeply connected to Pachamama—our beautiful Mother Earth below us. You also feel yourself deeply and equally connected to the cosmic wisdom that is above us—Father Sky—the presence and light of Inti the great sun.

As above, so below; we bring into our heart the union of the Divine Feminine and the Divine Masculine. These energies dance the dance of magic in our hearts and the music that they are dancing to is the music and frequency of love. And we are dancing into the portal, as we are entering this journey in a way that we have never experienced before. In this we discover that what is beyond the portal is filled with magic because it is connected to our own personal imagination, and it is also connected to the personal gifts that each one of us are meant to receive. So I invite you to feel your joy as the male and female within you are dancing within your heart, knowing that this is the key to opening it. See the portals of your heart opening and inviting you to walk through them.

As you are coming through, you see pathways, you see pure light—rainbow light, all colors of the rainbow. This rainbow light is the pathway that you are walking upon. These colors make up the beautiful flag of the Incan Empire, the rainbow flag that carries the full spectrum of light united in friendship to create the whole illumination for everyone to see and experience. This path is vibrating and guiding us to where we are to go. We trust this guidance from the light. We trust this guidance of the spirits of the Earth and we let these spirits guide us through.

Moving along the path of rainbow light, we find ourselves in a beautiful valley, the Sacred Valley of the Inca. Here everything grows with vitality and Mother Earth expresses herself in magical ways. We can see the plants and the mountains vibrating at a frequency that is pure light. We can see the aura of everything. We are in the valley sitting upon this beautiful field, which is made of sweetgrass. In front of us is a beautiful stone; this is our altar for the day. This beautiful stone in front of us is where we have our mesa—the mesa of our sacred journey. In Peru, a mesa is a paqo's altar. It is a bundled cloth that holds all of a paqo's sacred objects and tools of power. When a mesa is opened the spiritual medicine and energy of the paqo's sacred objects is shared with the world.

You approach the mesa and notice that the cloth is an ancient Peruvian cloth woven thousands of years ago by the medicine women of the Incan Empire. You are being called to open your mesa. There is power inside it that activates your memory of receiving your gifts of power from the different initiations you have gone through before. Your hands come and untie the mesa in a respectful way, and the mesa begins to present itself to you. As you open it, you notice the first thing that is coming to you is the beautiful skin of a snake.

You hold the snake skin within your hands and you remember the moment when the Great Serpent god Amaru gifted you with this skin; you remember the message you received from this powerful being and you connect with the energy of the Ukhu Pacha—receiving the gifts and wisdom from the Andean underworld. This wisdom from the underground is the ancient medicine of letting go, of releasing what is no longer serving us. As you hold this medicine in your hands right now, you think of everything that is in the present time that you are still holding on to, that is weighing on you, and that is not supporting you in being fully present for all the gifts of the moment. And you connect your heart to the heart of Mother Snake and you ask her to activate her medicine in you, into the wisdom of your heart so that you can feel the safety of letting go; you can feel the blessings of no attachment.

You feel this magical energetic process happening to your whole being where your own skin feels like falling off. All this dry, old skin—no longer supportive of who you are becoming—is just falling off of you and onto the ground. The ground—Mother Earth—is accepting your old skin as nutrients for her own land. Mother Earth is taking what you are letting go, what you shed, as nutrition for her flowers and her grass. You are fertilizing the earth with your old skin, which holds the power of all the lessons you've received in the past . . . You feel your new skin like a pink light of joy and rejuvenation fill your entire being. You thank Mother Snake and Ukhu Pacha for this opportunity.

Your hands begin to look for the next gift on your mesa and you find upon your mesa there is a beautiful paw of our sister, Puma. She is coming to you, and you see her eye to eye. Your eyes and her eyes are looking deep into one another. She is powerful and her presence is intense and there is so much sweetness as you dive deeply into her eyes. You feel her entering your body like you are channeling her and she is talking to you about the honor of walking upon the Earth, on Kay Pacha. And through her eyes you look around and you see Kay Pacha, the dimension of all that is around you, in a very different light. You are seeing this world from beauty, gratitude, and beyond.

You take a deep breath and you realize that Puma has brought you to the threshold where the world of the physical meets the world of the nonphysical. In this place, you feel connected and at peace with the world—accepting and understanding the flow and cosmic order of life. At this threshold, where the two worlds meet, you are able to see the world through the eyes of Puma, observing the world with the wisdom of Kay Pacha. You know that everything in life happens for a reason—a sacred purpose—and with this knowing a sense of peace fills your heart. You breathe in and allow this peace and wisdom to fill your body, inviting the spirit of Puma and the wisdom of Kay Pacha to reside within you.

Puma lives within you, the gift and the medicine of knowing where to put your paw and how to gently walk upon the Earth, guided by trust with each step. You feel yourself walking, gently allowing the unified field of love that is 360 degrees around you to hug you now and welcome you permanently to the awareness of Kay Pacha as the awareness of the divine plan. Here you know that everything that is inside of you will express itself outside you, so you feel a deep honoring and a deep responsibility to bring your attention to the inside and nurture and build within because that building is what is being reflected in your Kay Pacha. This relationship with your within and your without is in great harmony and constitutes a deep union of love, and you thank the beautiful puma for this opportunity to see and understand that this is so.

You feel your hands going to the mesa again looking for the next gift. And there you feel a beautiful, gentle, soft feather of Condor— this ancient, beautiful big brother who is in front of you carrying the wisdom of a lifetime. This condor feather is transmitting to you an entire life of flights. These are flights into high dimensions, which take you in this moment on the wings of freedom into Hanan Pacha, the high levels of consciousness. You fly with Condor and you know that the condor and its beautiful wings, when they spread and soar above all, understand everything in life from a higher perspective. And you feel your connection with the condor, as it gifts you right now the piece of seeing from above, where all the pieces of life touch together and fit perfectly with one another.

You can see the big picture of your life, the understanding as to why everything has been as it has been. And you trust that the future will unfold in the same divine order.

You feel Condor taking you even higher and you can see now the dimensions of this beautiful portal of the star people. Condor tells you in the heart that you are a star being, and the Hanan Pacha is your home, and you are bringing from the Hanan Pacha the ancient wisdom that is your blueprint into this lifetime. Condor is always here to fly with you to remember the origins of your soul. And you feel the stars and you as one and you feel the shining light within you, and you give thanks to the condor for taking you into this beautiful journey through Hanan Pacha.

You come back to the valley to the altar in front of you with deep gratitude for feeling one with all levels of consciousness that unite the Ukhu Pacha, the Kay Pacha, and the Hanan Pacha into your heart. You hold right here and now, within you, the gifts and the medicine of Snake, Puma, and Condor. You are feeling whole and complete, and you are in perfect coherence with your heart.

Within this space, you hear humming; an intense frequency surrounds you, and you see rings within rings of fluorescent light. Within this light you notice hundreds of little wings and realize that these wings are the origin of the humming frequency. As you watch the wings before you, you realize that these are the wings of hummingbirds. They move fast in the light and they create a vortex of magic around you. As you drop into this vortex of magic, a feeling comes over you that you can only describe as munay—the pure unconditional love of Creation. You are in the middle of this high frequency, and within your consciousness you know that you are in the presence of Korinti—the golden hummingbird. At this moment you experience no separation—there is nothing between you and Korinti. You breathe and you feel this connection within you. You know within your heart that at this moment you are the honey that is feeding the holy and divine presence of Korinti. You are the eye of the needle and you are the needle. You are the oneness and you are the one. You experience the nothing and the everything, and you know you have come to this expanded experience through the integration of all of the powers offered to you by the gifts within the mesa. You know you are in the joy and in the loving presence of Spirit. You breathe deeply, inhaling the joy of this moment, allowing this high vibration to fill your body and heart.

And you become present in your body and you become present in your heart. You come out of this beautiful journey to the awareness of your entire being, wherever you are sitting right now. You are feeling a new level of integration, feeling a new level of wholeness, and you breathe in and you breathe out. You are completely aware of your expansion and your intention to keep your experience alive, and you now have the medicine to support your everyday life.

And so it is.

THE CONDOR, THE EAGLE, AND THE PACHACUTEQ PROPHECY

AS I REFLECT UPON MY LIFE, I cannot help but be in complete amazement at how Spirit has moved and worked within it. Looking back, I can see how each step of my life (both positive and negative) has been used to support me in being where I am today—connected to the vision of the bigger picture and tethered to the path of my sacred purpose this lifetime. I truly believe there are no accidents in life. There is only the magic and mystery of Spirit, and when we open ourselves up to this infinite energy and say "yes!" to our holy longings, Spirit moves in our life in ways that we could not even begin to imagine.

As I shared in the introduction to this book, Chuma, the high priestess of Machu Picchu, came to me on my first visit to Peru. She called me toward my destiny and my sacred purpose, which is, as she informed me, to bring all the Children of the Sun back home. At the time, I had no idea what this meant. I had no idea how this purpose of mine would radically transform my life, the lives of others, and be an active component in fulfilling an ancient prophecy predicted many moons ago.

During this time in my life I was full of youth, passion, and vitality, and I also deeply trusted the mysteries of Spirit. So when I received Chuma's calling, I followed her guidance as a faithful servant—

questioning very little in the beginning, and then soon after questioning nothing at all. Chuma's calling activated a strong resonance within my heart and my spirit, and I could not ignore this feeling within me. At the time I felt I had only two options—jump out on a limb and follow Chuma's calling or play it safe and experience the remorse of missing out on my sacred purpose.

I took a chance and I jumped out on the limb offered to me. Saying yes to Chuma's call cost me my job, my security, and the comfort of a life rooted in predictability. But it has also given me a life deeply connected to Spirit, and over the past thirty-one years I have been able to witness and share the magic of the Andes Mountains with thousands of people from all over the world. To this day, I do not regret my decision to "jump," and I am grateful for my faith and my courage, which supported me in following the longings of my heart and soul.

Shortly after my first anniversary of leading journeys to Peru, Spirit called me to embark on yet another grand adventure—a move from Brazil to the United States. I must preface this by saying that moving to America was not a part of my life's plan. I never dreamed about relocating to the United States nor did I feel any inspiration to do so. Learning the English language was difficult for me and, honestly, the idea of leaving the comfort of Brazil was daunting.

When I received this calling to move to the United States, I did not want to go. But as I breathed and dropped into my heart, I knew it was what I had to do. By this time in my life I had already experienced the power of Spirit when we answer its call. I had already witnessed and been a recipient of Spirit's mysterious magic—receiving the envelope full of cash, which allowed me to embark on my first journey to Peru in 1989, and being supported to leave my job and start my own business facilitating spiritual journeys to Peru. These two experiences allowed me to trust and know that Spirit would guide and provide for me.

So, once again, I found myself jumping into the mysteries, following the call of Spirit. Moving from Brazil to the United States required me to leave my country, my family, my friends, my spiritual center, and all those that I loved and cared for. Spirit was guiding me to move to a country where I had no connections, no guaranteed success, and where

I would have to learn a completely new language as well as rebuild my business (and my life) from the ground up.

Again, registering all of this was daunting to me, yet I trusted Spirit and moved forward. I knew that Spirit was using me and my life in a grander and more divine way. Even though, at the time, I couldn't see the bigger picture and many things remained a mystery, I knew that this move was in accordance with the Divine's plan for my life.

I moved to the United States in July 1991. When I arrived I still had no idea why Spirit moved me here. As I was studying and learning how to speak English, Chuma came to me and provided me with the next step of my journey.

"You are to unite Brazilians and Americans and take them on a journey to Peru," Chuma announced to me.

"What!? How am I going to guide Americans? I cannot even speak their language!" I responded to Chuma.

Of course, Chuma was not one for humor. She is a demanding and focused spirit. Yet she has always been a guide and protector for me as I walk my path and follow my journey. So, once again, I took a deep breath and trusted the direction of Spirit's calling.

Before I knew it, I had a group of fourteen Americans and fourteen Brazilians signed up and ready to go to Peru. To this day I still do not know how the fourteen Americans discovered me or my journeys to Peru. After all, this was before the internet, cell phones, and email. What I do know is that we were all destined to travel to Peru, and Spirit brought us together.

Our group traveled to Peru in 1992. As I reflect upon this specific group, and this journey, I have to smile and laugh because we all encountered and experienced a language barrier. Personally, I would find myself getting confused. I would speak Portuguese to the Peruvians, English to the Brazilians, and Spanish to the Americans! My brain was disoriented, as it was my first experience being fully trilingual! The language barrier also occurred among the participants, yet they were still able to communicate with one another. The joy of being together allowed us all to navigate through the language barrier. As our journey to Peru continued I would find the Brazilians sharing a joke in Portuguese and the

Americans laughing in response. Other times, I would look at the group as we drove throughout Peru and I would see Brazilians and Americans looking at one another with tears streaming down their cheeks. No words were being exchanged yet they were fully communicating with each other—the language of the heart had superseded the language barrier and we were all using the language of love to communicate, connect, and recognize one another.

As we journeyed together and continued to merge with one another through our hearts, I witnessed our entire group undergo profound change and transformation while also growing closer in relationship to one another. At the time I did not understand how this union was possible; I found myself in the middle of a mystery.

I consulted with Don Pedrito, one of my lifelong friends and teachers, an Andean wisdom keeper and the first shaman I ever worked with in Peru.

Don Pedrito said to me, "You are the Condor of the South and the Americans are the Eagle of the North. We have been waiting for five hundred years for this time. It was predicted in the ancient prophecies: One day the Condor of the South and the Eagle of the North will come together and fly over the sky as one. When this happens, it is time to awaken the children of the Earth and build the bridge between the North and the South. You, Vera, must build this bridge."

I am supposed to build this bridge? I thought to myself. *How am I supposed to do this?*

I could not grasp Don Pedrito's message. I felt as if I were a child just wetting my toes in a giant pool full of mysteries, prophecies, and ancient wisdom.

Don Pedrito continued by saying, "Vera, you know the way of the heart. The way of the heart is the way of the Condor, and it is why you were sent to the North. You needed to go to North America to connect with their tribes and learn the way of the Eagle. It is important that they trust you and allow you within their ceremonies so that this unity between the two—the Eagle and the Condor—can happen.

"The Eagle of the North is one of the symbols for the masculine polarity. It governs the mind and mental wisdom. The Eagle of the

North has lived separated from the feminine ways of the heart, and we've reached a time upon our planet when these two energies must come together and unite. We must unite the wisdom of the mind with the wisdom of the heart, and in doing so we create the Yanantin-Masintin." Don Pedrito transmitted more of this prophecy to me.

Yanantin is a Quechua word that is defined as opposing pairs, or polarities, that continually merge with one another to create and sustain life. *Masintin* is the process of something new being created.

Don Pedrito continued to teach me, "Vera, you have a big mission but you are not alone. We are all here to support you as we all share this same mission. Our people knew this time would come; they predicted it in their prophecies many years ago. We have always known that one side of the pair—the Eagle and the Condor, the Masculine and the Feminine—always takes over and rules over the other, and right now this transition of energies is happening. When this great shift happens, a new cycle begins upon our planet. Our people call this new cycle—this new era—Pachacuteq. It is the era of change where yanantin (creation) is restored.

"Each cycle, or each Pachacuteq, lasts for about five hundred years. We are currently transitioning out of a cycle that has brought chaos and disorder. Within this last cycle our people experienced the destruction of our empire and the decimation of our lifestyle and sacred beliefs. We knew this time was coming and that it would be difficult and challenging, as death always precedes the birth of something new. Our ways have always taught us that we must walk through the dark night, and we must bring out all of the darkness that needs healing before we can rise into rebirth. When yanantin reemerges it will have undergone the changes and transformations needed to support the new era.

"The last cycle was overseen by our great avatar and leader Pachacuti Inca Yupanqui. He was the ninth Sapa Inca of Cuzco, and he transformed this kingdom into the Incan Empire. His name means 'transformer of the earth and cosmos,' as *pacha* means 'earth or cosmos' and *cuti* means 'to turn or correct, and to set things right.' Pachacuti was the man who built Machu Picchu and the Empire of the Children of the Sun. He was an architect of light and a visionary during an era of great transformation.

"At this time on our planet we need many Pachacutis to support and build the new era. This is no longer about us as a people—this prophecy predicts that this time upon our planet is transformative for everyone on Earth and all life within our universe. Our entire galaxy is in the end of times and we are transitioning into this next great era of consciousness. The 13,000-year cycle that our Mayan brothers and sisters spoke about completes soon, and that completion aligns with the transition of our own Pachacuteq. Now is the time for yanantin-masintin to be restored.

"Vera, look around you. You have fourteen condors and fourteen eagles here with you—a perfect balancing of opposites. When you bring them together as you have done, you have twenty-eight, which adds together to equal the number one. From a numerological standpoint, one is the number of new beginnings; it is the seed that is filled with the promises of new life. You can do this, Vera. Pachamama will support you, the spirits of the Earth will be your allies, and we will support you too.

"Even when the world becomes scary with destruction, do not be afraid. Can you imagine what it feels like for a baby leaving the womb? It must be a scary process, and yet the new life that it brings into the world is beautiful. The birth of new life is always preceded by contractions, and when the Earth has contractions she manifests them as earthquakes, volcanos, and other natural disasters. Right now, we are collectively in the period of contractions and we are trying to make our way to the birth canal of this new era. We are not there yet but we are slowly moving there.

"This collective death and rebirth that we are in is the transition from the masculine to the feminine. These next five hundred years will be guided by the Divine Feminine wisdom and the Cosmic Mother will take over. It is truly an honor to be alive at this time—we are the special ones chosen to support this great shift of the ages. We may not mentally know what it is we need to do, but the truth is that our inner wisdom knows—our soul knows and remembers its sacred purpose. All we need to do is know that and trust it. We will know what it is we need to do when our time comes. Trust this knowing, Vera. Trust."

Our conversation was enlightening, and through Don Pedrito's teachings I was beginning to obtain a bigger picture of my life. With his information I understood why Spirit asked me to leave my life in Brazil behind. I had to say yes to this calling because there was nowhere else for me to go but forward.

Here we are now in the year 2020—and, according to the ancient Andean prophecies, the Condor of the South and the Eagle of the North have been flying together since 1990. Since that time I have witnessed tremendous changes both within my life and also upon the planet. The first seven years I facilitated journeys to Peru, each group had a collective energy focused around releasing. These first groups worked heavily with Mother Snake and the Ukhu Pacha. We released and shed the skins of our past and found deep healing within the underworld by bringing our shadows to the light.

I remember clearly how my body of work (and the groups that I magnetized) moved from Ukhu Pacha to Kay Pacha. It was so clear to me how Puma took over—it even came to me in physical reality.

The year was 1996 and I was in Pisac. I had just arrived in my hotel and I was settling into my room when my guide called my room.

"I have a surprise for you. Come outside and see!" he said to me over the phone.

I rushed down to the receptionist deck and met my guide who was standing outside. Together we walked to a corner of the hotel's property where we discovered a big cage that was being protected. Inside the cage was a baby puma.

I could not believe my eyes. The hotel I was staying in had rescued a baby puma. The hotel staff shared with me that the puma's mother had died and they had found her baby roaming the mountains that surrounded the hotel property. At this time there were no sanctuaries or wildlife protection agencies available within this region of Peru. The hotel staff took it upon themselves to care for this little creature rather than let her wander the wilderness at such a vulnerable age and state.

The staff at the hotel allowed me the opportunity to hold the puma. I will never forget this experience—holding her filled my heart and body with tremendous love and connection. She wanted to be touched just like a baby cat. She wanted love, attention, and affection. While I was holding her I asked the staff if she had a name. The staff said no, and I took it upon myself to name this special being.

"Illa," I said. "Her name is Illa."

In Quechua, *illa* means light, and this little baby puma was definitely a light for me and my life, especially after I had spent the past seven years shedding, healing, and journeying through the underworld. Holding this little puma, I felt as though my journey through the Ukhu Pacha had come to completion. And as I reflect on the years following this experience, I can see how my own journey (as well as the journey shared by my groups) began to embody the recurring themes of spiritual strength, heart wisdom, and an understanding of how to use our intelligence for good—all of which are puma medicine.

Illa, the baby puma, remained onsite at this hotel for about a year. When I returned the following year she had grown and was too large for me to hold. Illa remembered me, though, and as I connected with her spirit she asked me to help free her—a request which I honored and completed. I contacted the Cuzco zoo and arranged for them to take Illa so that she could be cared for by trained professionals.

Since this experience, I have been able to witness the opening of several portals while facilitating journeys in Peru. I was in Peru for the opening of 08-08-2008, 09-09-2009, 11-11-2011, and 12-12-2012. Each of these dates provided an energetic portal that allowed our world to receive new levels of light, expanding our collective consciousness.

By the time our world reached the portal of 12-12-2012, I knew that our journey through the birth canal had begun. Pachacuteq was announcing the birth and the arrival of a new era of light. This new era is not a reemergence of who we have been in the past; it is a becoming of our future selves within the present moment. Throughout each of these portals leading up to 12-12-2012, I was guided by the spirit of Condor and I was able to gain a bigger picture of the trajectory behind this planetary transformation. I could see that humanity was indeed ready to receive the energy of the rising hummingbird. It was time to anchor the energy of joy, sweetness, and freedom upon the planet.

As I complete the writing of this book I find within myself a great hope for our planet. The 2020 COVID-19 pandemic has put the majority of humanity on a lockdown where we have been removed from our distractions. Earth and the Apurunas—the nature spirits—have begun renewing and restoring themselves. We have the opportunity now to become more aware of our relationship with Pachamama—Mother Earth. We have the chance to become more conscious of our impact upon the Earth, and we have the opportunity to remake ourselves. This is a time of rebirth for our planet and for humanity.

The light, the dark—there is no difference between the two. Both energies are portals that we can use to heal and transform. As I close the writing of this book and look at our global situation, I have to take a deep breath and allow the awe at what's happening upon our planet to sink in. Humanity was forced by nature to enter a sacred space where we could isolate and deal with ourselves, and reflect on our choices.

When I reflect and look at the actions of humanity before the 2020 pandemic, I see that we were all moving too fast. We were disconnected from the natural world, from each other, and from ourselves. We reached a new bottom—a rock bottom—and it is time to cultivate new values, reassess our priorities, and get real about what our needs really are. What really is essential for our lives to move forward in harmony, balance, and connection?

Pachamama spoke loudly, and humanity was placed within a period of isolation where we could reflect upon who we are as individuals and a collective. This time allowed us to journey within ourselves and reflect upon the following questions: Who are we? Why are we here? What is our purpose in life?

This pandemic has caused a great amount of change to surface within our mainstream society and around the world. I truly believe that we are moving into a new level of this initiation where choice is available. We can fully accept Earth's invitation to change, evolve, and enter the new era of light, or we can postpone for a little longer and continue to learn through pain and suffering. Regardless of our collective choice, planetary evolution and transformation will happen; we cannot avoid the quantum leap of who we are becoming.

If this book has found its way into your hands and heart, I want you to know that you are a part of this planetary transformation and evolution. You are a part of a cosmic star family that has incarnated upon planet Earth to support the expansion and evolution of consciousness. You are an ambassador of change. We are moving into the fifth level of consciousness and this vein of consciousness will be collective and soul-based. We will look with the eyes of our heart and, like the hummingbird, find great joy in the diversity upon our planet. Now is the time to remember your essence, and to remember what Don Pedrito said to me many moons ago, "We will need many Pachacutis to birth the new Earth, to be the transformers of the Above and the Below."

The shamanic mysteries of Peru can support us in awakening this new level of consciousness within ourselves. Journeying through the different pachas and working with the various energies found within can bring us into alignment with Earth. By carrying these teachings within your heart and opening yourself to the mysteries of the Andean cosmology you are answering the call of your own spirit and inner shaman. And by doing so, I trust that you will discover your part to play in this great, cosmic evolution and shift. Trust the wisdom of your heart, and allow it to guide your way.

HALLY!

VERA LOPEZ

APPENDIX

The Law of Ayni
in Action

THE AYNI PROJECT DEVELOPED from my desire to help the poor children of the Andes. It came into being quite organically, as an offshoot of my many trips to Peru. On these travels, I would frequently see very hungry children in the street at night and I would offer them what I could. I quickly realized that a little bit of material goods would go a long way for them, so I began to bring an abundance of basic necessities with me on my trips, which I would then distribute to the indigenous children.

Today when I travel to Peru with a group, we set aside one day to drive into the high altitudes of the Andes and spend the day in a village school connecting with these children. We bring our donations, which include blankets, socks, sweaters, gardening tools, lanterns, and other useful items that are not easily available to these people who are living so high up in the mountains. We also bring sweetbread and hot chocolate—two special (and rare) delicacies. We gift our donations to each of the children, and we watch their faces come alive as they receive them. They hug their blankets, put on their socks, eat their bread, and drink their hot chocolate. In return (and in alignment with ayni), they gift each of us with a bouquet of flowers harvested from their village— but in the larger picture, they gift us with so much more than that.

These children gift our hearts with an opportunity to experience firsthand the law of ayni. In our experience with them, they reflect back to us an essence of our own joy and purity. On the day that we experience the Ayni Project, we are able to remember how abundant we truly are, and we are able to provide joy to a community of people who, materially, have much less than we do.

Each of us has a special memory or a moment in time where we remember receiving a gift that made us feel special. This could be Christmas, a birthday, or another special holiday when you remember feeling absolutely loved, appreciated, and seen by someone who loved you. The Ayni Project creates this memory for these Andean children when we journey into these mountains and bring our gifts to them.

After visiting the same village for over thirty years, I have had the privilege to witness many of these children growing up and having children of their own. As they grow up, they still remember their experience with my groups coming into their schoolhouse with our gifts for them. They still hold on to this memory as one of the happiest times of their lives, keeping it stored within their hearts. Because of this I am passionate about the Ayni Project, and I recognize that it is a part of my own *kausay*—sacred purpose—this lifetime.

RESOURCES

SPIRITS OF THE EARTH
www.spiritsoftheearth.com

Founded and led by Vera Lopez, Spirits of the Earth creates, organizes, and guides spiritual journeys and retreats to sacred sites. It is also home to the Ayni Project and the Andean Mystery School.

Andean Mystery School

The Andean Mystery School is a highly experiential pathway that allows spiritual seekers the opportunity to study, connect with, and receive the shamanic mysteries of Peru. Participants learn how to astral travel and connect with the energies of the Incan temples and sacred sites. Receiving the karpay initiations of llankay, munay, and yachay allows individuals to activate the luminous seeds within their auric field. Compiling more than thirty years of direct experience, traditional study, and initiation, Vera Lopez guides journeyers through the mysteries of the Andes Mountains, supporting them in expanding their relationship with the archetypes and energies of shamanic Peru.

VENUS RISING ASSOCIATION FOR TRANSFORMATION
www.shamanicbreathwork.org

Founded by Linda Star Wolf, Ph.D., Venus Rising is dedicated to transforming personal and planetary consciousness during this great shifting of the ages, through Shamanic Breathwork and other tools of transformation and embodiment of Spirit. Venus Rising offers spiritual teachings, gatherings, celebrations, and ceremonies as well as university degree programs, training certifications, ministerial ordainment, retreats, and workshops around the world and at its home base in the blue mountains of North Carolina.

GLOSSARY

Andes Mountains: One of the world's largest mountain ranges, located in South America. These mountains stretch from the northern regions of Venezuela and pass through Ecuador, Peru, Bolivia, Argentina, Chile, and Colombia. They are believed to anchor the energies of the Divine Feminine on our planet Earth.

Ayni: The law of reciprocity, a highly revered principle and lifestyle in the Andes that is centered around giving and receiving.

Chakana (Incan Cross): *Chakana* means "to bridge" or "to cross." To the ancient Andean people, the Chakana was the sacred geometry of the Inca. Within its geometric shapes resides an energetic code—a transmission that shares how the shamans of the Andes view the universe and all the relationships in the cosmos. To the Andes people, the Chakana symbolically represents their principles and values, and it illustrates all the facets of the Andean cosmology.

coca leaves: A sacred plant found in the Andes and used by medicine men for ritual, ceremony, and healing.

cosmology: The systems and models of beliefs found in a culture. These systems and models detail the principles, values, and gods of a specific region, culture, and/or civilization.

Cuzco: The capital of the Incan Empire.

Hanan Pacha: The upper world of the Andean cosmology, ruled and guarded by Condor.

huayruro beads: Red and-black colored seeds that are used and worn by the Andean people for protection, grounding, and good luck.

Inca: The ancient civilization that founded and ruled the land known today as Peru.

Inti: The supreme god of the Inca and the creator god of the Andean cosmology; the sun and solar masculine force.

karpay: A series of initiations and light activations that are passed down through the Q'eros, generation after generation. The three karpays of the Q'eros are llankay, munay, and yachay.

Kay Pacha: The middle world of the Andean cosmology, ruled and guarded by Puma.

llankay: The first karpay of Q'eros initiations, it focuses on the pathway of service. The seeds of this initiation are kept within the three lower chakras.

Machu Picchu: The lost city of the Inca. Built by the ancient Inca as a university where high levels of spirituality were taught, this city anchored the celestial energies of the Star Nation onto planet Earth.

Mama Killa: The moon goddess of the Andean cosmology; this deity governs the feminine principle of the Q'eros belief system.

mesa: *Mesa* means "table" in Spanish. It can also refer to a sacred altar, or the bundle that the Incan and Q'eros priests and priestesses carry with them. This sacred piece of cloth holds and carries a shaman's power objects—sacred objects that are special to the specific shaman. Each object usually signifies an important initiation or life experience. While the objects within a mesa vary from shaman to shaman, the mesa itself is used within sacred ceremony, healing, divination, and prayer.

Moray: An ancient agricultural site in Peru. In the time of the Inca, the terrace gardens of Moray were used as laboratories where an Incan scientist would experiment with the growth of different crops.

munay: The second initiation or karpay in the Q'eros tradition; initiation focused around unconditional love, a principle that governs the heart and the flow of loving energy.

pacha: *Pacha* means "world" or "dimension" and represents a person's lifetime from birth to death.

Pachamama: Mother Earth of the Andes tradition, believed to be the spirit of the Earth and the Cosmic Mother, and the force that grants power to the shamans of Peru.

paqo: A Q'eros priest and/or shaman.

Q'eros: Nation/civilization of indigenous natives living in the high Andes of Peru. This nation was thought to have disappeared from the planet until they came down from the mountains in the early 1960s.

Quechua: The high vibrational language spoken by the Inca. This language is still alive today and it is spoken by the people of the Q'eros nation of Peru.

suyu: Suyu references the compass directions of North, East, South, and West.

Tawantinsuyu: The Incan Empire of the Four Directions.

Ukhu Pacha: The lower world, or underworld, of the Andean cosmology, ruled and guarded by the Great Serpent.

Yachay: The third karpay of the Q'eros tradition, the initiation of the great wisdom and higher perspective.

BIBLIOGRAPHY

Bellamy, Hans Schlindler, and Peter Allan. *The Calendar of Tiahuanaco: A Disquisition on the Time Measuring System of the Oldest Civilization in the World.* London: Faber & Faber, 1956.

Foerster, Brien. *Lost Ancient Technology of Peru and Bolivia.* Scotts Valley, Calif.: CreateSpace, 2013.

Krupp, E. C. *Echoes of the Ancient Skies: The Astronomy of Lost Civilizations.* Mineola, N.Y.: Dover Publications, 2003.

MacLaine, Shirley. *Out On a Limb.* New York: Bantam, 1986.

Mattimore, Carley, and Linda Star Wolf. *Sacred Messengers of Shamanic Africa: Teachings from Zep Tepi, the Land of First Time.* Rochester, Vt.: Bear & Co., 2018.

Melchizedek, Drunvalo. *Serpent of Light: The Movement of the Earth's Kundalini and the Rise of the Female Light, 1949–2013.* Newburyport, Mass.: Weiser Books, 2008.

Redfield, James. *The Celestine Prophecy: An Adventure.* New York: Grand Central Publishing, 2018.

Salazar, Fernando Elorrieta, and Edgar Elorrieta Salazar. *Cusco and the Sacred Valley of the Incas.* Cuzco, Peru: Tankar E.I.R.L., 2005.

Scully, Nicki, and Linda Star Wolf. *Shamanic Mysteries of Egypt: Awakening the Healing Power of the Heart.* Rochester, Vt.: Bear & Co., 2007.

Star Wolf, Linda. *Shamanic Breathwork: Journeying beyond the Limits of the Self.* Rochester, Vt.: Bear & Company, 2009.

Stone, Rebecca. *Art of the Andes: From Chavín to Inca.* London: Thames & Hudson, 2012.

INDEX

Page numbers in *italics* indicate illustrations

BOOKS OF RELATED INTEREST

Shamanic Breathwork
Journeying beyond the Limits of the Self
by Linda Star Wolf, Ph.D.
Foreword by Nicki Scully

Soul Whispering
The Art of Awakening Shamanic Consciousness
by Linda Star Wolf, Ph.D., and Nita Gage, DSPS, MA

Visionary Shamanism
Activating the Imaginal Cells of the Human Energy Field
by Linda Star Wolf and Anne Dillon

Shamanic Mysteries of Egypt
Awakening the Healing Power of the Heart
by Nicki Scully and Linda Star Wolf

The Anubis Oracle
A Journey into the Shamanic Mysteries of Egypt
by Nicki Scully and Linda Star Wolf

Power Animal Meditations
Shamanic Journeys with Your Spirit Allies
by Nicki Scully

Speaking with Nature
Awakening to the Deep Wisdom of the Earth
by Sandra Ingerman and Llyn Roberts

Sacred Energies of the Sun and Moon
Shamanic Rites of Curanderismo
by Erika Buenaflor, M.A., J.D.

INNER TRADITIONS • BEAR & COMPANY
P.O. Box 388 • Rochester, VT 05767
1-800-246-8648 • www.InnerTraditions.com

Or contact your local bookseller